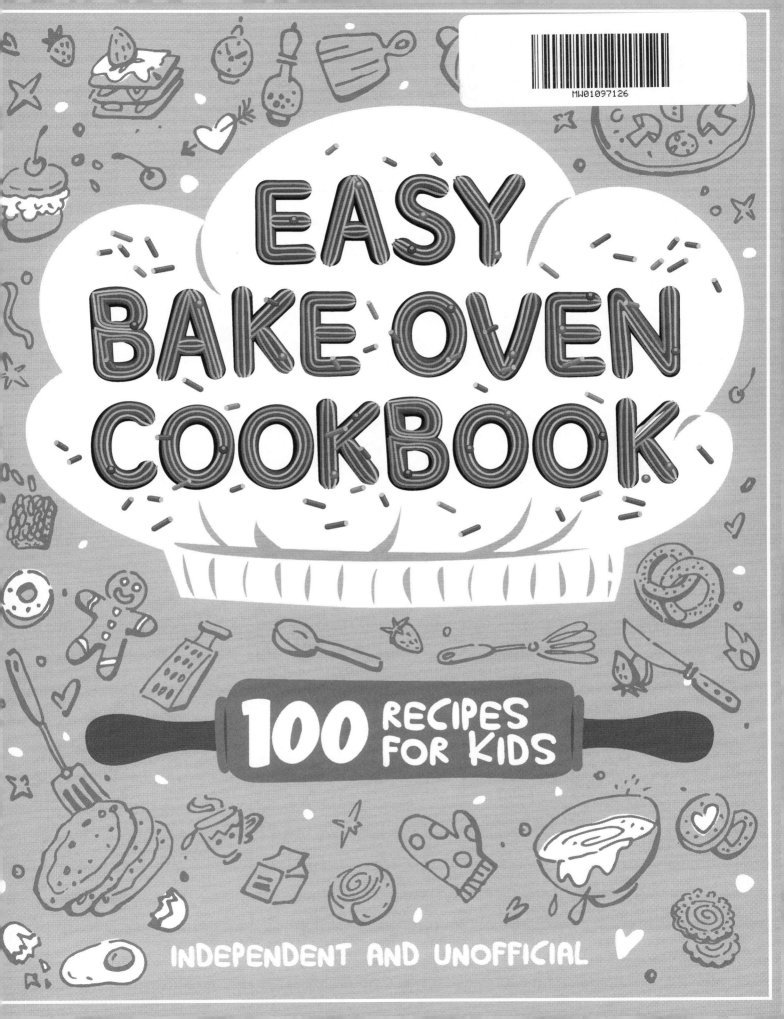

EASY BAKE OVEN COOKBOOK

100 RECIPES FOR KIDS

INDEPENDENT AND UNOFFICIAL

CONTENTS

INTRODUCTION

Welcome, little baker! We hear you're exploring the world of cooking and need some recipes to inspire your baking. This cookbook contains 100 recipes for your toy oven, ranging from easy to advanced, for all types of cooks. Whether you're creating a yummy afternoon snack or whisking up a sweet treat, you're sure to find something that fits your craving. Some bakers prefer to cook from scratch, while others prefer using box and pre-made mixes, so we've offered a little of both for everyone. The recipes are divided into sections for cookies, cakes from scratch, box-cakes, frostings and glazes, breakfast items, snackables, seasonal favorites, and some miscellaneous treats. If you get stuck along the way, remember that adults are great at providing help. It's also a good idea for an adult to be nearby whenever you're using the oven.

Keep in mind that these recipes were primarily tested with a typical, rectangular toy-baking pan, so using other dishes may result in different portion sizes. Also, while toy ovens are great for practicing your baking skills, sometimes they require a little troubleshooting. For example, some bakers find that their dishes only cook well on one side of the oven. If this happens to you, try rotating your pan halfway through your baking time so that the contents bake evenly on both sides. We've included this tip in some of the recipes in case you forget.

Finally, please remember to always follow proper baking instructions when using your toy oven. Have fun with your cooking!

CLASSIC CHOCOLATE CHIP COOKIES

INGREDIENTS

- ➢ 2 teaspoons of cold butter
- ➢ 3 tablespoons of flour
- ➢ ⅛ teaspoon of baking powder
- ➢ A small pinch of salt
- ➢ 2 teaspoons of white sugar
- ➢ 2 teaspoons of brown sugar
- ➢ 1 ½ teaspoons of milk
- ➢ ¼ teaspoon of vanilla extract
- ➢ ½ tablespoon of chocolate chips

INSTRUCTIONS

1. Preheat your toy oven and spray your baking sheet with nonstick cooking spray.
2. Mix flour, baking powder, and salt together in a bowl.
3. In a separate bowl, mix together the butter, milk, vanilla, brown sugar and white sugar.
4. Combine the ingredients by pouring the flour mixture into the butter and sugar mixture. Mix everything together until a dough forms.
5. You may need to use your hands a bit for this part to help form the dough and make sure everything is mixed together.
6. Mix the chocolate chips into the batter.
7. Roll the dough so that it forms tiny round balls. They should be about the size of a nickel or a quarter.
8. Arrange 6 cookies on the tray to bake. Flatten the tops of your cookies by pressing on them with your thumb. You want them to be small enough to fit through the oven's opening!
9. Bake for 6 minutes. Then carefully remove them from the oven, and rotate your pan so that the cookies cook evenly on the other side. Be careful not to touch the pan since it will be hot!
10. Bake the cookies for 6 more minutes, then remove them from the oven to cool for 2-3 minutes.

SNICKERDOODLE COOKIES FROM SCRATCH

INGREDIENTS

- ➤ 2 teaspoons of soft butter
- ➤ 2 teaspoons of light brown sugar
- ➤ 1 teaspoon of applesauce
- ➤ ½ teaspoon of vegetable oil
- ➤ 2 tablespoons of flour
- ➤ ⅛ teaspoon of baking powder
- ➤ ⅛ teaspoon of cream of tartar
- ➤ 1 teaspoon of white granulated sugar
- ➤ ¼ teaspoon of cinnamon

INSTRUCTIONS

1. Preheat your toy oven and spray your baking sheet with nonstick cooking spray.
2. Mix together the butter, brown sugar, applesauce and vegetable oil in a small bowl.
3. In a separate bowl, mix the flour, baking powder and cream of tartar.
4. Combine the two mixes by stirring the flour mixture into butter and sugar mixture.
5. The mix should thicken like cookie dough.
6. Roll the dough into tiny little balls that are roughly the size of a nickel.
7. In a separate bowl, mix together the white granulated sugar and cinnamon.
8. Roll the balls of cookie dough in the sugar and cinnamon mixture.
9. Arrange 6 cookies on the tray to bake.
10. Press the tops of your cookies with your thumb.
11. You'll want to make sure your cookies will be small enough to fit into the oven's opening.
12. Bake for 12 minutes. Tip: For more evenly baked cookies, rotate your pan after 6 minutes. Remove the pan from the oven and put it back in for another 6 minutes with the pan facing the opposite direction.
13. Allow your cookies to cool a few minutes before eating.

MINT CHIP COOKIES

INGREDIENTS

- 3 tablespoons of flour
- ⅛ teaspoon of baking powder
- 1 tablespoon of cold butter
- 1 teaspoon of white sugar
- 2 tablespoons of brown sugar
- ½ teaspoon of mint extract
- 1 ½ teaspoons of milk
- 2 drops of green food coloring
- 1 tablespoon of mini chocolate chips

INSTRUCTIONS

1. Preheat your toy oven and spray your baking sheet with nonstick cooking spray.
2. Mix flour and baking powder together in a small bowl.
3. In a separate bowl, mix together the butter, white and brown sugars, milk, mint extract, and green food coloring.
4. Now you can combine the mixtures by adding the flour to the bowl of butter and sugar.
5. Mix everything together. You may need to use your hands a bit for this part.
   The batter should thicken and form a dough.
6. Add the chocolate chips and mix them into the batter.
7. Roll the dough into tiny little balls.
8. Arrange 6 of them on the tray to bake.
9. Press the tops of your cookies with your thumb before putting them in the oven so that they fit. They should be about the size of a thick quarter.
10. Bake for 7 minutes. Then carefully remove them from the oven, and rotate your pan so that the cookies cook evenly on the other side. Be careful not to touch the pan since it will be hot! Bake the cookies for 7 more minutes, then remove them from the oven to cool.

SUGAR COOKIES

INGREDIENTS

- ➢ 2 teaspoons of butter
- ➢ 3 teaspoons of sugar
- ➢ 2 drops of vanilla extract
- ➢ 1 teaspoon of applesauce
- ➢ 2 tablespoons of flour
- ➢ ¼ teaspoon of baking powder

INSTRUCTIONS

1. Preheat your toy oven and spray your baking sheet with nonstick cooking spray.
2. Mix together butter and sugar in a small bowl.
3. Add the vanilla and applesauce to the butter mixture and stir.
4. Sprinkle in the flour and baking powder. Stir everything together.
5. The mix should thicken and form a dough. You may need to use your hands a bit for this part until a dough forms.
6. You can either store your batter in a sealed container in the fridge to use for later, or cook them now.
7. To bake your cookies, roll the dough into 12 equal little balls and arrange 6 of them on the tray to bake.
8. The cookies should be roughly the size of a quarter.
9. Bake for 6 minutes. Then carefully remove them from the oven, and rotate your pan so that they cook evenly on the other side. Be careful not to touch the pan since it will be hot!
10. Bake the cookies for 6 more minutes, then remove them from the oven to cool.

JAM THUMBPRINT COOKIES

INGREDIENTS

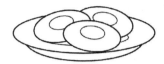

➢ Refrigerated, sugar cookie dough (reference "Sugar Cookies" recipe)
➢ 3 teaspoons of strawberry jam

INSTRUCTIONS

1. Preheat your toy oven and spray your cooking pan with non-stick cooking oil.
2. Slice off a piece of your cookie dough and form four little circles, roughly the size of a quarter.
3. Arrange your cookies on the pan.
4. Using the tip of your pinky finger, make a tiny indent in the middle of each cookie.
5. Use the end of a small spoon to drop just enough jam inside to fill the hole. Be careful not to overfill them.
6. Bake for 6 minutes.
7. Carefully rotate your pan and let the cookies finish baking on the other side for another 5 minutes. Remember to use a pot holder, the pan will be hot!
8. Allow your cookies a few minutes to cool before eating.

BIRTHDAY CAKE COOKIES

INGREDIENTS

- ➤ 3 tablespoons of Vanilla Box Cake Mix
- ➤ 1 tablespoon of flour
- ➤ ½ tablespoon of vegetable oil
- ➤ ½ tablespoon of rainbow sprinkles
- ➤ 2 teaspoons of applesauce
- ➤ 1 tablespoon powdered sugar

INSTRUCTIONS

1. Preheat your toy oven and spray your baking sheet with nonstick cooking spray.
2. Mix flour, vanilla cake mix, sprinkles, vegetable oil and applause into a bowl until a dough forms. If the dough is too sticky, you can sprinkle a teaspoon of flour into the batter.
3. Roll the dough into 12 little equal sized balls.
4. Sprinkle the powdered sugar onto a plate.
5. Roll the cookies in powdered sugar.
6. Arrange 6 cookies on the tray to bake and flatten the tops of them with a spoon so that they are roughly the size of a quarter.
7. Bake for 5 minutes.
8. Carefully remove them from the oven, and rotate your pan so that the cookies cook evenly on the other side. Be careful not to touch the pan since it will be hot!
9. Bake the cookies for 5 more minutes, then remove them from the oven to cool 2-3 minutes.

GINGERSNAP COOKIES

INGREDIENTS

- ➢ 3 tablespoons of flour
- ➢ ¼ teaspoon of baking powder
- ➢ ¼ teaspoon of ground ginger
- ➢ ¼ teaspoon of cinnamon
- ➢ 1 ½ tablespoons of sugar
- ➢ 1 ½ teaspoons of milk
- ➢ 1 teaspoon of dark molasses
- ➢ 1 tablespoon of soft butter

INSTRUCTIONS

1. Preheat your toy oven and spray your baking sheet with nonstick cooking spray.
2. Mix the flour, baking powder, ginger, cinnamon and salt in a small bowl.
3. In a separate bowl, mix together the butter, sugar, milk and molasses.
4. Carefully combine the two mixtures and stir everything together.
5. The mix should begin to thicken like dough. You may need to use your hands a bit to help form the dough into one large, round ball of dough.
6. Break off some dough and make tiny little balls for your cookies.
7. The cookies should be roughly the size of a thick quarter.
8. Arrange your cookies so that there are 6 cookies on the tray and have enough space to bake. Press the top of your cookies with your thumb.
9. Bake for 6 minutes. Then carefully remove them from the oven, and rotate your pan so that the cookies cook evenly on the other side. Be careful not to touch the pan since it will be hot!
10. Bake the cookies for 6 more minutes, then remove them from the oven to cool.

LEMON CAKE COOKIES

INGREDIENTS

- ➢ 3 tablespoons of Lemon Box Cake Mix
- ➢ 1 tablespoon of flour
- ➢ ½ tablespoon of vegetable oil
- ➢ ½ teaspoon of lemon extract
- ➢ 2 teaspoons of applesauce
- ➢ 1 tablespoon of powdered sugar

INSTRUCTIONS

1. Preheat your toy oven and spray your baking sheet with nonstick cooking spray.
2. Mix flour, lemon box cake mix, lemon extract, vegetable oil and applesauce into a bowl until a dough forms. If the dough is too sticky, you can sprinkle a teaspoon of flour into the batter.
3. Roll the dough into little equal sized balls.
4. Sprinkle the powdered sugar onto a plate.
5. Roll the cookies in powdered sugar.
6. Arrange 6 cookies on the tray to bake and flatten the tops of them with a spoon so that they are roughly the size of a quarter.
7. Bake for 5 minutes.
8. Carefully remove them from the oven, and rotate your pan so that the cookies cook evenly on the other side. Be careful not to touch the pan since it will be hot!
9. Bake the cookies for 5 more minutes, then remove them from the oven to cool 2-3 minutes.

TRADITIONAL PEANUT BUTTER COOKIES

INGREDIENTS

- ➢ 1 tablespoon of peanut butter
- ➢ ½ tablespoon of cold butter
- ➢ ½ tablespoon of white sugar
- ➢ ½ tablespoon of brown sugar
- ➢ 2 tablespoons of flour
- ➢ ⅛ teaspoon of baking powder
- ➢ 2 teaspoons of milk
- ➢ 2 drops of vanilla extract

INSTRUCTIONS

1. Preheat your toy oven and spray your baking sheet with nonstick cooking spray.
2. In a small bowl, mix the butter, peanut butter, vanilla extract, sugars and milk.
3. In a separate bowl, mix the flour and baking powder together.
4. Add the flour mixture and stir everything together. You may need to use your hands to help the dough form.
5. Make 6 little balls of dough and place them onto your greased baking sheet.
6. Arrange them so that they have enough space to bake. Your cookies should be roughly the size of a thick quarter.
7. Using a fork, criss-cross the tops of your cookies by flattening them with the prongs of a fork. They should be flat with a pattern on top when you're finished.
8. Bake for 5 minutes.
9. Carefully remove them from the oven, and rotate your pan so that the cookies cook evenly on the other side. Be careful not to touch the pan since it will be hot!
10. Bake the cookies for 5 more minutes, then remove them from the oven to cool 2-3 minutes.

MONSTER COOKIES

INGREDIENTS

- ➢ 1 ½ teaspoons of peanut butter
- ➢ 2 tablespoons of flour
- ➢ 1 tablespoon of oats
- ➢ ⅛ teaspoon of baking powder
- ➢ 2 teaspoons of white sugar
- ➢ 2 ½ teaspoons of milk
- ➢ 1 teaspoon of mini M&M's
- ➢ 1 teaspoon of chocolate chips

INSTRUCTIONS

1. Preheat your toy oven and spray your baking sheet with nonstick cooking spray.
2. Mix flour, oats, baking powder, and sugar together in a bowl.
3. Add the peanut butter. Then slowly add the milk and stir everything together. The mix should thicken like cookie dough. You may need to use your hands a bit for this part.
4. Last, mix in the M&Ms and chocolate chips.
5. Roll the dough into little balls and place them on the tray to bake. Make sure they have enough room to bake and are small enough to fit inside the oven!
6. Repeat this until there are 4 balls of cookie dough total.
7. Press your cookies with your thumb to flatten their tops.
8. They should be about the size of a thick quarter.
9. Bake for 6 minutes. Then carefully remove them from the oven, and rotate your pan so that the cookies cook evenly on the other side. Be careful not to touch the pan since it will be hot!
10. Bake the cookies for 6 more minutes, then remove them from the oven to cool.

OATMEAL RAISIN COOKIES

INGREDIENTS

- ➢ 1 ½ tablespoons of flour
- ➢ 2 ½ tablespoons of rolled oats
- ➢ ⅛ teaspoon of baking powder
- ➢ ¼ teaspoon of cinnamon
- ➢ 2 teaspoons of cold butter
- ➢ 1 teaspoon of white sugar
- ➢ 2 teaspoons of brown sugar
- ➢ 2 teaspoons of milk
- ➢ ½ tablespoon of raisins

INSTRUCTIONS

1. Preheat your toy oven and spray your baking sheet with nonstick cooking spray.
2. Mix flour, oats, baking powder, cinnamon and sugars together in a bowl.
3. Add the butter, then slowly add the milk. Stir everything together and the batter should begin to thicken like cookie dough. Use your hands to help roll or pat the dough together.
4. Add the raisins and mix them into the dough.
5. Shape your cookies by making 6 little balls of dough and arrange them on the tray to bake.
6. Press the tops of your cookies with your thumb so they are flat enough to fit inside the oven. They should be about the size of a thick quarter.
7. Bake for 6 minutes. Then carefully remove them from the oven, and rotate your pan so that the cookies cook evenly on the other side. Be careful not to touch the pan since it will be hot!
8. Bake the cookies for 6 more minutes, then remove them from the oven to cool.

WHITE CHOCOLATE PEANUT COOKIES

INGREDIENTS

- ➢ 2 teaspoons of cold butter
- ➢ 3 tablespoons of flour
- ➢ ⅛ teaspoon of baking powder
- ➢ 2 teaspoons of white sugar
- ➢ 2 teaspoons of brown sugar
- ➢ 1 ½ teaspoons of milk
- ➢ ½ tablespoon of white chocolate chips
- ➢ 2 teaspoons of diced peanut pieces

INSTRUCTIONS

1. Preheat your toy oven and spray your baking sheet with nonstick cooking spray.
2. Mix flour, baking powder, and sugars together in a bowl.
3. Add the butter, vanilla extract and milk. Stir everything together and the mix should thicken like cookie dough. You may need to use your hands a bit for this part.
4. Mix in the white chocolate chips and peanuts last.
5. Roll the dough into little balls and place them on the tray to bake.
6. Place six cookies on the pan to bake.
7. Press the tops of your cookies with your thumbs so that they fit inside the oven.
8. The cookies should be roughly the size of a thick quarter.
9. Bake cookies for 7 minutes.
10. Carefully remove them from the oven, and rotate your pan so that the cookies cook evenly on the other side. Be careful not to touch the pan since it will be hot!
11. Bake the cookies for 7 more minutes, then remove them from the oven to cool 2-3 minutes.

CHOCOLATE CAKE FROM SCRATCH

INGREDIENTS

➢ 1 ½ tablespoons of flour
➢ 2 teaspoons of sugar
➢ 1/8 teaspoon of baking powder
➢ 2 teaspoons of butter
➢ 1 pinch of salt
➢ 1 ½ teaspoons of cocoa powder
➢ 2-3 teaspoons of milk
➢ Chocolate sprinkles for the top

INSTRUCTIONS

1. Preheat your toy oven and spray your baking sheet with non-stick cooking oil.
2. In a small bowl, mix together flour, sugar, baking powder, cocoa powder and salt.
3. Then, add the butter and mix well.
4. Add the milk slowly until the consistency is smooth and creamy.
5. Pour the batter evenly into your sprayed pan.
6. Bake for 7 minutes.
7. Carefully remove your pan from the oven and bake for another 7 minutes with the pan facing the opposite direction. This way your cake will cook evenly on both sides.
8. Once your cake has cooled, you can decorate your cake with your favorite frosting flavor (refer to "Frostings" section of this cookbook) and top with sprinkles.

CARROT CAKE FROM SCRATCH

INGREDIENTS

- ➢ 2 tablespoons of plain flour
- ➢ 2 tablespoons of brown sugar
- ➢ 1/4 teaspoon of baking powder
- ➢ 1/4 teaspoon of cinnamon
- ➢ 1 pinch of nutmeg
- ➢ 1 small pinch of salt
- ➢ 1 teaspoon of vegetable oil
- ➢ 1 tablespoon of milk
- ➢ 1 baby carrot, shredded
- ➢ Refrigerated "Cream Cheese Frosting" (recipe included in this book)

INSTRUCTIONS

1. Preheat your toy oven and spray your cooking pan with oil.
2. In a small bowl, mix together the flour, sugar, baking powder, spices and salt.
3. Add the oil and milk to the mixture and give it a good stir.
4. Add the shredded carrot and pecans to the bowl and mix.
5. Spread the batter into your sprayed cooking pan. Be careful not to overfill the pan!
6. Follow your oven's directions and bake for 7 minutes.
7. Using an oven mit, remove your pan and place it back in the oven so that it faces the opposite direction. Bake for another 7 minutes so that it cooks both sides evenly.
8. Remove your cake from the oven and let it cool a few minutes before decorating.
9. This cake's flavor goes nicely with cream cheese frosting (refer to "Cream Cheese Frosting" recipe), but you can choose any icing or frosting recipe to decorate it.

RASPBERRY WHITE CHOCOLATE CAKE FROM SCRATCH

INGREDIENTS

- ➢ 2 tablespoons of flour
- ➢ 1 tablespoon of sugar
- ➢ 1/8 teaspoon of baking soda
- ➢ 1 tablespoon of butter
- ➢ 1 small pinch of salt
- ➢ 1 tablespoon of milk
- ➢ 1 tablespoon of fresh raspberries
- ➢ 1 tablespoon of white chocolate chips (melted)

INSTRUCTIONS

1. Preheat your toy oven and spray your cooking pan with non-stick cooking oil.
2. In a small bowl, mix together flour, sugar, baking soda and salt.
3. Then, have an adult help you melt white chocolate chips in the microwave for 30 seconds.
4. Pour the melted white chocolate into the bowl of flour and sugar.
5. Add the butter and milk and stir until the consistency is smooth and creamy.
6. Stir in the raspberries.
7. Spread the batter evenly on your sprayed cooking pan.
8. Bake for 8 minutes.
9. Remove your pan and place it back in the oven for another 8 minutes, this time with the pan facing the opposite direction so that it cooks evenly.
10. Allow the cake a few minutes to cool before eating.

APPLE SPICE CAKE FROM SCRATCH

INGREDIENTS

- ➤ 1 ½ tablespoons of flour
- ➤ 2 teaspoons of white sugar
- ➤ ¼ teaspoon of baking powder
- ➤ 2 teaspoons of allspice
- ➤ 1 teaspoon of cold butter
- ➤ 1 teaspoon of applesauce
- ➤ 1 tablespoon of minced apples
- ➤ 1 teaspoon of milk

INSTRUCTIONS

1. Preheat your toy oven and spray your cooking pan with nonstick cooking oil.
2. Have an adult help you peel and dice the apple into tiny little pieces.
3. In a small bowl, mix together the flour, sugar, allspice and baking powder.
4. Mix in the butter until the consistency resembles a crumbly texture. You may want to use your hands to mix everything together.
5. Add the applesauce into the bowl.
6. Add the milk. Stir until the consistency is smooth and creamy.
7. Stir in your apple pieces.
8. Pour the batter evenly into your greased pan. (Be careful not to overfill the pan!)
9. Bake for a total of 16 minutes. For a more evenly baked cake, rotate your pan after 8 minutes so that it bakes evenly on both sides.
10. Once your cake has cooled, you can decorate it.
11. Choose a frosting recipe for your cake and carefully follow the recipe's directions (refer to "Frostings" section in this cookbook).
12. Pour the frosting on top of the cake and enjoy.

CARAMEL CAKE FROM SCRATCH

INGREDIENTS

- ➢ 2 tablespoons of flour
- ➢ 1 ½ teaspoons of brown sugar
- ➢ ¼ teaspoon of baking powder
- ➢ 1 pinch of salt
- ➢ 3 teaspoons of butter
- ➢ 1 teaspoon of corn syrup
- ➢ 2 teaspoons of milk
- ➢ 1 tablespoon of caramel sauce
- ➢ ½ teaspoon of coarse sea salt (optional)

INSTRUCTIONS

1. Preheat your toy oven and spray your baking pan with nonstick cooking oil.
2. In a small bowl, mix together flour, sugar, baking powder and salt.
3. Then, add the butter and mix well.
4. Add the vanilla. Slowly add the milk and stir until the consistency is smooth and creamy.
5. Pour the batter evenly into your baking sheet.
6. Bake for a total of 16 minutes. For a more evenly cooked cake, rotate your cake after 8 minutes so that it bakes evenly on both sides.
7. Once your cake has cooled, you can decorate it.
8. Make the chocolate frosting to turn this into a salted caramel cake, or choose your own frosting flavor to make (refer to "Frostings" section in this cookbook).
9. Spread the chocolate frosting on top of the cake and sprinkle some coarse sea salt on top.

VICTORIAN VANILLA CAKE FROM SCRATCH

INGREDIENTS

- ➢ 2 tablespoons of flour
- ➢ 1 ½ teaspoons of white granulated sugar
- ➢ 1/8 teaspoon of baking powder
- ➢ 2 tablespoons of butter
- ➢ Pinch of salt
- ➢ 1 tablespoon of applesauce
- ➢ 4 teaspoons of milk
- ➢ 2 drops of vanilla extract

INSTRUCTIONS

1. Preheat your oven and spray your cooking pan with nonstick cooking spray.
2. In a small bowl, mix together flour, sugar, baking powder and salt.
3. Then, add the chilled butter and mix well.
4. Add the applesauce and vanilla. Then add the milk slowly and stir until the consistency is smooth and creamy.
5. Add the batter to your sprayed cooking pan.
6. Follow the oven's instructions and bake for 9 minutes.
7. Carefully remove the cake from the oven and rotate the pan so that it cooks evenly on the other side for another 9 minutes.
8. Once the cake is finished baking and cooled, mix up your favorite icing or frosting flavor to decorate your cake (refer to "Frostings" section in this cookbook).

PUMPKIN CAKE FROM SCRATCH

INGREDIENTS

- ➢ 1 ½ tablespoons of flour
- ➢ 2 teaspoons of sugar
- ➢ ¼ teaspoon of baking powder
- ➢ 2 ½ teaspoons of butter
- ➢ ¼ teaspoon of nutmeg
- ➢ 1 tablespoon of pumpkin
- ➢ 1 ½ teaspoons of milk

INSTRUCTIONS

1. Preheat your toy oven and spray your baking sheet with non-stick cooking oil.
2. In a small bowl, mix together flour, sugar, baking powder, nutmeg and salt.
3. Then, add the butter and mix well.
4. Stir in the milk and pumpkin. The consistency will be slightly fluffy when everything is all mixed in.
5. Pour the batter evenly into your sprayed pan.
6. Bake for 7 minutes.
7. Carefully remove your pan from the oven and bake for another 7 minutes with the pan facing the opposite direction. This way your cake will cook evenly on both sides.
8. Once your cake has cooled, you can decorate your cake with a cream cheese frosting or add another favorite frosting flavor (refer to "Frostings" section in this cookbook).

RED VELVET CAKE FROM SCRATCH

INGREDIENTS

- ➢ 2 tablespoons of flour
- ➢ 2 tablespoons of white granulated sugar
- ➢ ¼ teaspoon of baking powder
- ➢ ½ tablespoon of cocoa powder
- ➢ 1 tiny pinch of salt
- ➢ 1 teaspoon of vegetable oil
- ➢ 1 tablespoon of milk
- ➢ ¼ teaspoon of white distilled vinegar
- ➢ ¼ teaspoon of red food coloring
- ➢ Refrigerated cream cheese frosting "Frostings and Glazes" recipes

INSTRUCTIONS

1. Preheat your toy oven and spray your cooking pan with nonstick cooking spray.
2. In a small bowl, mix together the fbur, sugar, baking powder, salt and cocoa powder.
3. Then, in a separate bowl, add the milk and white vinegar and stir. Add the vegetable oil, and red food coloring to the bowl and stir it all up until the red color its all blended up.
4. Add the red mixture to the fbur mixture by slowly stirring in the fbur.
5. Slowly add the batter to your sprayed cooking pan. Be careful to leave some space on top so the pan doesn't get too full!
6. Bake for 8 minutes.
7. When its fnished, remove the pan from the oven and rotate your pan so that it cooks evenly on the other side for an additional 8 minutes.
   Make sure you use a pot holder, the pan will be hot!
8. Carefully remove the pan from the oven and let the cake cool before decorating it.
9. Once the cake has cooled, spread the cream cheese frosting over the top of the cake.

BIRTHDAY CAKE FROM SCRATCH

INGREDIENTS

- ➤ 2 tablespoons of flour
- ➤ 3 teaspoons of white sugar
- ➤ ¼ teaspoon of baking powder
- ➤ A tiny pinch of salt
- ➤ 3 teaspoons of butter
- ➤ 1 tablespoon of milk
- ➤ 1/4 teaspoon of vanilla extract
- ➤ 1 tablespoon of applesauce
- ➤ 1 tablespoon of rainbow sprinkles

INSTRUCTIONS

1. Preheat your toy oven and spray your baking pan with nonstick cooking oil.
2. In a small bowl, mix together flour, sugar, baking powder and salt.
3. Then, add the butter and mix until the contents resemble a gritty, sand texture. You may want to use your hands to make sure it's mixed together.
4. Add the vanilla. Slowly add the milk and stir until the consistency is smooth and creamy.
5. Stir in the sprinkles.
6. Pour the batter evenly into your baking sheet.
7. Bake for a total of 16 minutes. For a more evenly cooked cake, rotate your cake after 8 minutes so that it bakes evenly on both sides.
8. Once your cake has cooled, you can decorate it.
9. Choose a frosting recipe for your cake and carefully follow the recipe's directions (refer to "Frostings" section of this cookbook).
10. Spread the frosting on top of the cake and enjoy.

FIZZY LEMONADE CAKE FROM SCRATCH

INGREDIENTS

- ➢ 2 tablespoons of flour
- ➢ 3 teaspoons of sugar
- ➢ ¼ teaspoon of baking soda
- ➢ 3 tablespoons of butter
- ➢ 1 pinch of salt
- ➢ ½ teaspoon of lemonade drink mix
- ➢ 1 ½ tablespoons of milk

INSTRUCTIONS

1. Spray cooking pan with non-stick cooking oil.
2. In a small bowl, mix together flour, sugar, baking soda, lemon drink mix and salt.
3. Then, add the butter and mix well.
4. Add the milk slowly until the consistency is creamy.
5. Spread the batter evenly on your sprayed cooking pan.
6. Follow the instructions on your toy and bake for 12-14 minutes.

FIZZY STRAWBERRY-DRINK CAKE FROM SCRATCH

INGREDIENTS

- ➢ 2 tablespoons of flour
- ➢ 3 teaspoons of sugar
- ➢ ¼ teaspoon of baking soda
- ➢ 1 teaspoon butter
- ➢ 1 pinch of salt
- ➢ ½ teaspoon of strawberry drink mix
- ➢ 1 ½ tablespoons of milk

INSTRUCTIONS

1. Spray your cooking pan with nonstick cooking oil.
2. In a small bowl, mix together flour, sugar, baking soda, strawberry drink mix and salt.
3. Then, add the butter and mix well.
4. Add the milk slowly until the consistency is smooth and creamy.
5. Spread the batter evenly on your sprayed cooking pan.
6. Follow instructions on your toy oven and bake for a total of 18 minutes. If you want your cake to cook more evenly, rotate the pan about halfway through your bake time.

GINGERBREAD CAKE FROM SCRATCH

INGREDIENTS

- ➤ 2 tablespoons of flour
- ➤ 2 tablespoons of brown sugar
- ➤ ¼ teaspoon of baking powder
- ➤ ¼ teaspoon of ground ginger
- ➤ ¼ teaspoon of ground cloves
- ➤ 1 small pinch of salt
- ➤ 1 teaspoon of butter
- ➤ 1 ½ teaspoon molasses
- ➤ 1 tablespoon of milk

INSTRUCTIONS

1. Preheat your toy oven and spray your cooking pan with non-stick cooking oil.
2. In a small bowl, mix together flour, baking powder, ginger, cloves and salt.
3. In a separate bowl, combine the butter, brown sugar, molasses and milk.
4. Slowly add the flour mixture into the other bowl by stirring occasionally until everything is all mixed up.
5. Spoon the batter into your sprayed cooking pan. Be careful to leave some space at the top so the pan doesn't get too full!
6. Bake for 8 minutes.
7. When it's finished, remove the pan from the oven and rotate your pan so that it cooks evenly on the other side for an additional 8 minutes.
   Make sure you use a pot holder, the pan will be hot!
8. Carefully remove the pan from the oven and let the cake cool before eating.

MILK CHOCOLATE BOX CAKE

INGREDIENTS

➢ 2 ½ tablespoons of Betty Crocker Milk Chocolate cake mix
➢ 1 tablespoon of applesauce
➢ 1 teaspoon of milk
➢ 1 teaspoon of oil
➢ 2 teaspoons of chocolate sprinkles

INSTRUCTIONS

1. Preheat your toy oven and spray your cooking pan with non-stick cooking oil.
2. In a small bowl, combine the cake mix, applesauce, oil and milk.
3. Mix until all the ingredients are fully combined.
4. Spoon the batter evenly onto your sprayed cooking pan.
   Be careful to leave a little space on top so that the cake doesn't overflow.
5. Follow your toy oven's instructions and bake for 14 minutes.
6. For a more evenly baked cake, rotate the pan after 7 minutes so that it cooks well on both sides. Be careful not to burn yourself, the pan will be very hot!
7. Once the cake has cooled, you can cover it with your favorite frosting (refer to "Frostings" section of this cookbook) and top it with sprinkles to finish it off.

TRADITIONAL VANILLA BOX CAKE

INGREDIENTS

- ➤ 2 ½ tablespoons of Pillsbury Vanilla Cake Mix
- ➤ 1 tablespoon of applesauce
- ➤ 1 teaspoon of milk
- ➤ 1 teaspoon of oil
- ➤ 1-2 drops of vanilla extract

INSTRUCTIONS

1. Preheat your toy oven and spray your cooking pan with non-stick cooking oil.
2. In a small bowl, mix together the cake mix, applesauce, milk and vanilla.
3. Mix everything together until the consistency is smooth.
4. Spoon the batter evenly onto your sprayed cooking pan. Be careful to leave a little space on top so that the cake doesn't overflow.
5. Bake for 12-14 minutes.
6. For a more evenly baked cake, rotate the pan after it's cooked for 7 minutes.
   This way it cooks well on both sides. Be careful not to burn yourself, the pan will be very hot!
7. Once the cake has cooled, use your favorite frosting recipe (refer to "Frostings" section of this cookbook) and spread it on top of the cake.

LAYERED DEVIL'S FOOD BOX CAKE (ADVANCED)

INGREDIENTS

- ➤ 3 tablespoons of Pillsbury Devil's Food Premium Cake Mix
- ➤ 1 tablespoon of applesauce
- ➤ 1 teaspoon of oil
- ➤ ½ tablespoon of milk
- ➤ Refrigerated Chocolate Buttercream Frosting (recipe in this cookbook)

INSTRUCTIONS

1. Preheat your toy oven and spray your cooking pan with non-stick cooking oil.
2. In a small bowl, combine the cake mix, applesauce, oil and milk. Give it a good stir until everything is blended together.
3. Spoon the batter evenly onto the cooking pan.
4. Bake for 8 minutes.
5. Carefully remove the pan from the oven and place it back in the oven for another 8 minutes, this time so the pan faces the opposite direction. Be careful not to burn yourself, the pan will be very hot.
6. Let the cake cool for 2-3 minutes.
7. Once the cake is cooled completely, get an adult to help you cut it in half.
8. Spread some of your chocolate buttercream frosting on one half of the cake, then carefully place the other half on top.
9. Cover the top of the cake with the rest of the frosting and enjoy!

FUNFETTI BOX CAKE

INGREDIENTS

- ➤ 2 ½ tablespoons of Pillsbury Funfetti Cake Mix
- ➤ 1 tablespoon of applesauce
- ➤ 1 teaspoon of vegetable oil
- ➤ 1 teaspoon of milk
- ➤ 1 teaspoon of rainbow sprinkles for the top
- ➤ Refrigerated Vanilla Frosting (recipe in this cookbook)

INSTRUCTIONS

1. Preheat your toy oven and spray your cooking pan with non-stick cooking oil.
2. In a small bowl, add the cake mix, applesauce, oil, and milk. Stir it all together.
3. Spoon the batter evenly into the greased cooking pan. Be careful to leave a little space on top so that the cake doesn't overflow.
4. Follow your toy oven's cooking directions and bake for 14 minutes.
5. For a more evenly baked cake, rotate the pan after 7 minutes so that it cooks evenly on both sides. Be careful not to burn yourself, the pan will be very hot!
6. Remove the cake from the oven and let it cool for 2-3 minutes before decorating.
7. Cover the top of the cake with vanilla frosting and top with sprinkles.

RED VELVET BOX CAKE

INGREDIENTS

- ➢ 2 ½ tablespoons of Betty Crocker Red Velvet Cake Mix
- ➢ 1 tablespoon of applesauce
- ➢ 1 teaspoon of water
- ➢ 1 teaspoon of oil
- ➢ 2 teaspoons of red sprinkles
- ➢ Cream Cheese Frosting (recipe in this cookbook)

INSTRUCTIONS

1. Preheat your oven and spray your cooking pan with non-stick cooking oil.
2. In a small bowl, combine the cake mix, applesauce and water. Mix well until all of the ingredients are fully combined.
3. Spoon the batter evenly on your sprayed cooking pan. Be careful to leave a little space on top so that the cake doesn't overflow.
4. Follow your oven's instructions for cooking and bake for 16 minutes.
5. For a more evenly baked cake, rotate the pan after 8 minutes so that it cooks well on both sides. Be careful not to burn yourself, the pan will be very hot!
6. Let the cake finish cooking on the other side for the remaining 8 minutes.
7. Once the cake has cooled, cover it with cream cheese frosting and top with sprinkles.

BUTTER PECAN BOX CAKE

INGREDIENTS

- ➢ 2 ½ tablespoons of Betty Crocker Butter Pecan Cake Mix
- ➢ 1 tablespoon of applesauce
- ➢ 2 teaspoons of water
- ➢ 1 teaspoon of room temperature butter
- ➢ 1 tablespoon of chopped pecans

INSTRUCTIONS

1. Preheat your toy oven and spray your cooking pan with non-stick cooking oil.
2. In a small bowl, combine the cake mix, applesauce and water.
3. Mix until all of the ingredients are fully combined.
4. Spoon the batter evenly onto your sprayed cooking pan. Be careful to leave a little space on top so that the cake doesn't overflow.
5. Follow your toy oven's instructions for baking and cook for 12-14 minutes. For a more evenly cooked cake, rotate the pan after 7 minutes so that it cooks well on both sides.
6. Once the cake has cooled, cover the top and sides of the cake with the frosting of your choice (refer to "Frostings" section in this cookbook). Sprinkle the chopped nuts over the frosting to finish.

CHERRY CHIP BOX CAKE

INGREDIENTS

- ➢ 3 tablespoons of Betty Crocker Cherry Chip Cake Mix
- ➢ 1 tablespoon of applesauce
- ➢ 1 teaspoon of water
- ➢ 1 teaspoon of oil

INSTRUCTIONS

1. Preheat your toy oven and spray the cooking pan with non-stick cooking oil.
2. In a small bowl, combine the cake mix, applesauce, water and oil.
3. Mix well until all of the ingredients are fully combined.
4. Carefully spoon the batter into your greased cooking pan. Be careful not to fill it too full!
5. Bake for a total of 16 minutes. For a more evenly cooked cake, rotate your cake after 8 minutes so that it bakes evenly on both sides.
6. Remove from the oven and set aside to cool.
7. Once the cake has cooled, use your favorite frosting recipe (refer to the "Frostings and Glazes" section of this cookbook) and spread it on top of the cake.

CINNAMON BUN FLAVORED BOX CAKE

INGREDIENTS

- ➢ 2 tablespoons of Pillsbury Cinnamon Bun Flavored Cake Mix
- ➢ 1 tablespoon of applesauce
- ➢ 1 teaspoon of cream cheese
- ➢ 1 teaspoon of water
- ➢ A small pinch of cinnamon
- ➢ Premade Cream Cheese Frosting (recipe in this cookbook)

INSTRUCTIONS

1. Preheat your oven and spray your cooking pan with non-stick cooking oil.
2. In a small bowl, combine the cake mix, applesauce, cream cheese, water and cinnamon. Mix well until all of the ingredients are fully combined.
3. Spoon the batter evenly on your sprayed cooking pan.
4. Follow the instructions on your toy oven and bake for 12-14 minutes.
5. For a more evenly baked cake, rotate the pan at 6 minutes so that it cooks well on both sides. Be careful and use a potholder, the pan will be hot!
6. Once the cake has cooled, cover the top of the cake with some cream cheese frosting and enjoy!

PINEAPPLE FLAVORED
BOX CAKE

INGREDIENTS

- ➤ 2 ½ tablespoons of Pillsbury Pineapple Cake Mix
- ➤ 1 tablespoon of applesauce
- ➤ 1 teaspoon of vegetable oil
- ➤ 1 teaspoon of pineapple juice
- ➤ 1 teaspoon of milk

INSTRUCTIONS

1. Preheat your toy oven and spray your cooking pan with non-stick cooking oil.
2. In a small bowl, mix together the cake mix, milk, applesauce, vegetable oil and pineapple juice.
3. Mix everything together until your cake batter is smooth and creamy.
4. Spoon the batter evenly into your sprayed cooking pan. Be careful to leave a little space on top so that the cake doesn't overflow.
5. Bake for 12-14 minutes.
6. For a more evenly baked cake, rotate the pan after it's cooked for 7 minutes.
   This way it cooks evenly on both sides. Be careful not to burn yourself, the pan will be very hot!
7. Once the cake has cooled, choose a frosting recipe (included in this cookbook) to decorate your cake.
8. Cover the top of the cake with your favorite flavor and enjoy!

LEMON FLAVORED BOX CAKE

INGREDIENTS

- ➤ 2 tablespoons of Betty Crocker Super Moist Lemon Cake Mix
- ➤ 1 tablespoon of applesauce
- ➤ 1 tablespoon of water
- ➤ 1 teaspoon of room temperature butter
- ➤ Prepared "Lemon Glaze" (recipe included in this book)

INSTRUCTIONS

1. Preheat your toy oven and spray your cooking pan with non-stick cooking oil.
2. In a small bowl, combine lemon cake mix, applesauce, butter and water.
3. Mix until all of the ingredients are fully combined.
4. Spoon the batter evenly onto your sprayed cooking pan.
5. Bake for 6 minutes.
6. Carefully rotate the pan and bake for another 6 minutes so that the cake cooks well on both sides. Be careful to use a potholder since the pan will be hot!
7. Once the cake has cooled, mix up a yummy lemon glaze or another frosting flavor to top your cake with.

PUMPKIN FLAVORED BOX CAKE

INGREDIENTS

- ➢ 2 tablespoons of Pillsbury Pumpkin Premium Cake Mix
- ➢ 1 tablespoon of applesauce
- ➢ 1 teaspoon of cream cheese
- ➢ 2 ½ teaspoons of milk
- ➢ 1 teaspoon of oil
- ➢ 1/4 teaspoon of cinnamon
- ➢ Refrigerated "Cream Cheese Frosting" (recipe included in this book)

INSTRUCTIONS

1. Preheat your toy oven and spray your cooking pan with non-stick cooking oil.
2. In a small bowl, combine the pumpkin cake mix, applesauce, cream cheese, milk, oil and cinnamon.
3. Mix well until all of the ingredients are fully combined and there are no more lumps in the batter.
4. Spoon the batter evenly onto your sprayed cooking pan. Be careful to leave some space from the top so that it doesn't overflow in the oven!
5. Follow your oven's cooking instructions and bake for 15 minutes.
6. For a more evenly baked cake, rotate your pan after 7 minutes so that it cooks well on both sides. Be careful to use a potholder because the pan will be hot!
7. Remove from the oven and let the cake cool for a few minutes.
8. Once the cake has cooled, top the cake with some cream cheese frosting or another frosting flavor of choice.

VANILLA FROSTING

INGREDIENTS

- ➤ 3 teaspoons of soft butter
- ➤ 4 teaspoons of powdered sugar
- ➤ ¼ teaspoon of vanilla extract
- ➤ ¼ teaspoon of milk

INSTRUCTIONS

1. Mix together the butter and powdered sugar in a small bowl.
2. Stir in the vanilla and milk. Mix well until the frosting is soft and creamy, and all the ingredients are fully combined.
3. If your frosting feels a little stiff, add a drop of milk. If it is too runny, slowly add an extra teaspoon of powdered sugar.
4. Leave the frosting to chill in the fridge until you're ready to use it.

CHOCOLATE BUTTERCREAM FROSTING

INGREDIENTS

- ➢ 3 teaspoons of melted chocolate
- ➢ 4 teaspoons of soft butter
- ➢ 2 tablespoons of powdered sugar
- ➢ ¼ teaspoon of cocoa powder
- ➢ ¼ teaspoon of milk

INSTRUCTIONS

1. Mix together the butter and powdered sugar in a small bowl.
2. Have an adult help you melt the chocolate in the microwave.
3. Add the cocoa powder and milk to the butter and sugar.
4. Stir in the melted chocolate.
5. Mix until the frosting is soft and creamy.
6. If your frosting feels a little stiff, add a drop of milk. If it is too runny, add an extra teaspoon of powdered sugar.
7. Leave the frosting to chill in the fridge until you're ready to use it.

STRAWBERRY FROSTING

INGREDIENTS

➢   3 teaspoons of butter
➢   4 teaspoons of powdered sugar
➢   2 teaspoons of strawberry syrup or jam
➢   A drop of red food coloring (optional)

INSTRUCTIONS

1. Mix together the butter and powdered sugar in a small bowl.
2. Stir in the milk, strawberry syrup and food coloring. Mix well until the frosting is soft and creamy, and all the ingredients are fully combined.
3. If your frosting feels a little stiff, add a drop of milk. If it is too runny, slowly add an extra teaspoon of powdered sugar.
4. Leave the frosting to chill in the fridge until you're ready to use it.

PEANUT BUTTER FROSTING

INGREDIENTS

- ➢ 3 teaspoons of butter
- ➢ 2 tablespoons of powdered sugar
- ➢ 3 teaspoons of peanut butter
- ➢ A tiny pinch of salt (optional)

INSTRUCTIONS

1. Mix together the butter and powdered sugar until they are light and fluffy.
2. Stir in the peanut butter and salt. Mix well until the frosting is soft and creamy, and all the ingredients are fully combined.
3. If your frosting feels a little stiff, add a drop of milk. If it is too runny, slowly add half a teaspoon of powdered sugar until it thickens.
4. Leave the frosting to chill in the fridge until you're ready to use it.

CREAM CHEESE FROSTING

INGREDIENTS

➢ 3 teaspoons of cream cheese
➢ 2 teaspoons of powdered sugar
➢ 1-2 drops of vanilla extract
➢ ½ teaspoon of milk

INSTRUCTIONS

1. Mix together the cream cheese, milk, powdered sugar and vanilla.
2. Stir everything together until there are no more lumps.
3. If your frosting feels a little stiff, add ¼ teaspoon of milk and mix it in. If it is too runny, slowly add an extra teaspoon of powdered sugar.
4. Leave the frosting to chill in the fridge until you're ready to use it.

BLUEBERRY FROSTING

INGREDIENTS

- ➤ 4 teaspoons of soft butter
- ➤ 4 teaspoons of powdered sugar
- ➤ ¼ teaspoon of milk
- ➤ 3-4 blueberries
- ➤ A drop of blue food coloring

INSTRUCTIONS

1. Mix together the butter and powdered sugar in a small bowl.
2. Get an adult to help you mash up the blueberries with a spoon.
3. Stir the milk and food coloring into the butter mixture. Then stir in the blueberries.
4. Mix well until the frosting is soft and creamy, and all the ingredients are fully combined.
5. If your frosting feels a little stiff, add a drop of milk. If it is too runny, slowly add an extra teaspoon of powdered sugar.
6. Leave the frosting to chill in the fridge until you're ready to use it.

CARAMEL FROSTING

INGREDIENTS

- ➢ 3 teaspoons of soft butter
- ➢ 4 teaspoons of powdered sugar
- ➢ 2 teaspoons of caramel sauce

INSTRUCTIONS

1. Mix together the butter and powdered sugar in a small bowl.
2. Stir in the caramel sauce. Mix well until the frosting is soft and creamy, and all the ingredients are fully combined.
3. If your frosting feels a little stiff, add a drop of milk. If it is too runny, slowly add an extra teaspoon of powdered sugar and stir.
4. Leave the frosting to chill in the fridge until you're ready to use it.

MARSHMALLOW FROSTING

INGREDIENTS

➢   4 teaspoons of marshmallow fluff
➢   2 teaspoons of soft butter
➢   2 tablespoons of powdered sugar
➢   ¼ teaspoon of milk

INSTRUCTIONS

1.   Mix together the butter and powdered sugar in a small bowl.
2.   Stir the marshmallow fluff into the butter mixture.
3.   Add in the milk, and mix well until the frosting is soft and creamy.
4.   If your frosting feels a little stiff, add a drop of milk. If it is too runny, slowly add an extra teaspoon of powdered sugar.
5.   Leave the frosting to chill in the fridge until you're ready to use it.

MINT FROSTING

INGREDIENTS

- ➤ 3 teaspoons of butter
- ➤ 2 tablespoons of powdered sugar
- ➤ 1-2 drops of green food coloring
- ➤ ¼ teaspoon of pure mint extract
- ➤ ½ teaspoon of milk

INSTRUCTIONS

1. Mix together the butter and powdered sugar in a small bowl.
2. Stir in the green food coloring, mint extract and milk.
3. Mix well until the frosting has a creamy green consistency, and all the ingredients are fully combined.
4. If your frosting feels a little stiff, add a drop of milk. If it is too runny, slowly add an extra teaspoon of powdered sugar.
5. Leave the frosting to chill in the fridge until you're ready to use it.

WHITE CHOCOLATE FROSTING

INGREDIENTS

- ➤ 2 teaspoons of white chocolate chips, melted
- ➤ 3 teaspoons of soft butter
- ➤ 4 teaspoons of powdered sugar
- ➤ ¼ teaspoon of milk (optional)

INSTRUCTIONS

1. Mix together the butter and powdered sugar in a small bowl.
2. In a separate bowl, have an adult help you microwave the white chocolate chips by placing them in the microwave for 40 seconds. Stir the white chocolate with a spoon and heat for another 40 seconds if not melted.
3. Add the melted white chocolate to the butter and sugar mixture.
4. Mix until the frosting is soft and creamy, and all the ingredients are fully combined.
5. If your frosting feels a little stiff, add the milk. If it is too runny, add an extra teaspoon of powdered sugar to thicken it up.
6. Leave the frosting to chill in the fridge until you're ready to use it.

COOKIE ICING

INGREDIENTS

- ➢ 2 tablespoons of powdered sugar
- ➢ ¼ teaspoon of light corn syrup
- ➢ 1 teaspoon of milk
- ➢ ¼ teaspoon of vanilla extract
- ➢ 1-2 drops of your favorite food coloring

INSTRUCTIONS

1. Mix together the powdered sugar, vanilla, corn syrup and milk in a small bowl.
2. You can divide your icing into separate bowls to make different colors, or make one color.
3. Add a drop of food coloring and mix until you have your icing color.
4. If your icing feels a little stiff, add ¼ teaspoon of milk. If it is too runny, add an extra teaspoon of powdered sugar until it reaches the thickness you'd like.
5. Use the icing to decorate your cookies, and then let the icing dry before eating.

VANILLA GLAZE

INGREDIENTS

- ➤ 2 tablespoons of powdered sugar
- ➤ ¼ teaspoon of butter
- ➤ ½ teaspoon of milk
- ➤ 1 drop of vanilla extract

INSTRUCTIONS

1. Mix together the butter and powdered sugar in a small bowl.
2. Add the vanilla and milk.
3. Mix until a runny consistency forms.
4. If your glaze feels a little stiff, add a drop of milk. If it is too runny, add an extra teaspoon of powdered sugar until it reaches the thickness you'd like.
5. Drizzle the glaze over your treat when you're ready to use it.
   Tip: You can add glazes to some sweet treats or breakfast dishes to add a yummy flavor.

LEMON GLAZE

INGREDIENTS

- ➤ 2 tablespoons of powdered sugar
- ➤ ¼ teaspoon of butter
- ➤ ½ teaspoon of milk
- ➤ 1-2 drops of lemon extract
- ➤ 1 drop of yellow food coloring (optional)

INSTRUCTIONS

1. Mix together the butter and powdered sugar in a small bowl.
2. Add the lemon extract and milk.
3. Mix until a runny consistency forms.
4. If your glaze feels a little stiff, add ¼ teaspoon of milk. If it is too runny, add an extra teaspoon of powdered sugar until it reaches the thickness you'd like.
5. Drizzle the glaze over your treat when ready to use it.
   Tip: For a splash of color, add a drop of yellow food coloring or leave it plain.

BREAKFAST QUESADILLA

INGREDIENTS

- ➢ 2 mini flour tortillas
- ➢ 1-2 teaspoons grated cheddar cheese
- ➢ ½ tablespoon of bacon bits
- ➢ 2 teaspoons of canned, boston baked beans
- ➢ Side of sour cream and ketchup (optional)

INSTRUCTIONS

1. Preheat your toy oven and spray your cooking pan with oil.
2. Have an adult help to trim the tortillas down to size so that they fit the width of your pan.
3. You should have two identical mini circles that fit inside your cooking pan.
4. Place one of your mini tortillas onto the pan.
5. Cover one tortilla with the cheese and beans.
6. Add the bacon on top.
7. Layer the other tortilla on top to form your quesadilla.
8. Follow the instructions on your toy oven and bake for 10 minutes.
9. Remove from the oven and allow your quesadilla a few minutes to cool.
10. Enjoy with a side of sour cream or ketchup.

BAKED FRENCH TOAST

INGREDIENTS

- ➢ 1 thin slice of white or sourdough bread
- ➢ 1 egg, beaten
- ➢ 1 tablespoon of milk
- ➢ 2 tablespoons of brown sugar
- ➢ ⅛ teaspoon of cinnamon
- ➢ ½ teaspoon of powdered sugar
- ➢ 1 tablespoon of maple syrup (optional)

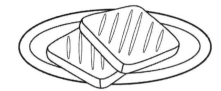

INSTRUCTIONS

1. Preheat your toy oven and spray your cooking pan with oil.
2. Have an adult help you trim off the crust of the bread.
3. With a small butter knife cut the bread down the middle so that there are two halves side by side.
4. Next, cut the bread in half again so that you have four equal parts.
   Tip: If your bread is larger than some and won't fit onto the pan, you can cut your bread again so that you have little rectangular pieces.
5. In a small bowl, mix together the egg, milk, brown sugar, and cinnamon.
6. Cover your bread pieces with the egg mixture by dunking them into the bowl.
7. Arrange a couple pieces of bread onto the baking pan.
8. Follow instructions on your toy oven and cook for 15 minutes.
9. Remove from the oven and let your french toast cool for a few minutes.
10. Serve your french toast with a dusting of powdered sugar or your favorite syrup.

CHOCOLATE CHIP PANCAKES

INGREDIENTS

- ➤ 1 tablespoon of egg, beaten
- ➤ 1 tablespoon of milk
- ➤ 1 ½ tablespoons of flour
- ➤ 1 teaspoon of sugar
- ➤ ⅛ teaspoon of baking soda
- ➤ ½ teaspoon of butter, softened
- ➤ 1 tablespoon of mini chocolate chips
- ➤ 1 tablespoon of syrup (optional)

INSTRUCTIONS

1. Preheat your toy oven and spray your cooking pan with oil.
2. In a small bowl, whisk together the egg, butter and milk.
3. In a separate bowl, combine the flour, baking soda, and sugar.
4. Whisk the mixture until fully combined.
5. Slowly add the flour mixture to the bowl with egg and milk mixture and stir everything together.
6. Stir in the chocolate chips.
7. Spoon ½ tablespoon of the batter on one side of the pan.
8. Repeat on the other side so that you have two uncooked pancakes side by side.
9. Follow the instructions on your toy oven and cook for 6 minutes.
10. Have an adult help you rotate the pan and place it back in the oven for another 6 minutes.
11. Remove from the oven and allow the pancakes to cool for a few minutes before eating.
12. Enjoy with some of your favorite syrup.

BANANA NUT BREAKFAST CAKE

INGREDIENTS

- ➤ 2 tablespoons of melted butter
- ➤ 3 teaspoons of white sugar
- ➤ ½ tablespoon of applesauce
- ➤ 1 ½ tablespoons of flour
- ➤ ¼ teaspoon of baking soda
- ➤ A small pinch of salt
- ➤ 1 inch of fresh banana
- ➤ ¼ teaspoon of cinnamon
- ➤ 2 teaspoons of brown sugar
- ➤ 1 tablespoon of chopped walnuts or pecans

INSTRUCTIONS

1. Preheat your toy oven and spray your cooking pan with oil.
2. Divide the melted butter by scooping 3 teaspoons of melted butter into a separate bowl. Set one bowl aside for later.
3. Add the white sugar to the bowl of butter and stir.
4. Next, add the applesauce, white sugar, baking soda and salt into the bowl of butter and sugar.
5. Stir everything together.
6. Use a fork to mash the banana. Add the banana to the batter and mix well.
7. Add the flour, milk, and nuts. Stir everything together.
8. Pour your batter into the sprayed cooking pan and set aside while you make the topping.
9. Using the remaining bowl of butter, add the brown sugar and stir.
10. Drizzle the topping over the pan.
11. Follow the instructions on your toy oven and cook for 8 minutes.
12. Have an adult help you remove the pan from the oven and place it back in so that it faces the opposite direction.
13. Cook for another 8 minutes.
14. Remove the pan and allow a few minutes to cool before eating.

BANANA PANCAKE

INGREDIENTS

- ➢ 1 inch of banana
- ➢ 1 tablespoon of milk
- ➢ 2 tablespoons of flour
- ➢ 1 teaspoon of sugar
- ➢ ¼ teaspoon of ground cinnamon
- ➢ A tablespoon of peanut butter or maple syrup for topping

INSTRUCTIONS

1. Preheat your toy oven and spray your cooking pan with oil.
2. In a small bowl, mash up the banana with a fork.
3. Stir the milk, flour, sugar and cinnamon into the banana mixture.
4. Stir the mixture with a spoon until fully combined.
5. Scoop out ½ a tablespoon of pancake mix and place it on one side of the pan.
6. Repeat so that there are two spoonfuls of pancake batter side by side.
7. Bake for 12 minutes.
8. For more evenly cooked pancakes, have an adult help you rotate the pan after 6 minutes and place it back in the oven for another 6 minutes.
9. Remove from the oven and allow a few minutes to cool before eating.
10. You can enjoy your pancakes with peanut butter or syrup.

BLUEBERRY BREAKFAST MUFFIN

INGREDIENTS

- ➢ 1 tablespoon of blueberries
- ➢ 2 ½ tablespoons of flour
- ➢ 2 teaspoons of sugar
- ➢ ⅛ teaspoon of baking soda
- ➢ 1 pinch of salt
- ➢ 3 teaspoons of chilled butter
- ➢ 1 teaspoon of milk
- ➢ 1 teaspoon of plain yogurt

Vanilla Icing:

- ➢ 2 tablespoons of powdered sugar
- ➢ ¼ teaspoon of butter
- ➢ ½ teaspoon of milk
- ➢ 1 drop of vanilla extract

INSTRUCTIONS

1. Spray your pan with nonstick cooking oil.
2. In a small bowl, mix together the flour, sugar, baking soda and salt.
3. Then, add the butter and mix well.
4. Add the milk and yogurt slowly until the consistency is smooth and creamy. Then stir in the blueberries.
5. Pour the batter evenly into the pan.
6. Follow instructions on your toy oven and bake for 6 minutes.
7. Rotate your pan and bake for another 6 minutes so that it cooks evenly on both sides.
8. While the cake is baking, make the icing. Combine the powdered sugar, butter, milk and vanilla in a bowl and stir everything together.
9. When the breakfast cake has finished baking, use a spoon to drizzle the icing on top and enjoy.

MAPLE BACON BREAKFAST CAKE

INGREDIENTS

- ➤ 1 ½ tablespoons of flour
- ➤ ¼ teaspoon of baking powder
- ➤ 1 small pinch of salt
- ➤ 1 ½ teaspoons of butter
- ➤ 2 teaspoons of white sugar
- ➤ 1 ½ teaspoons of plain yogurt
- ➤ 1 teaspoon of milk
- ➤ 2 teaspoons of maple syrup
- ➤ 1 tablespoon of bacon bits

INSTRUCTIONS

1. Preheat your toy oven and spray your cooking pan with nonstick cooking spray.
2. In a small bowl, mix together the flour, sugar, baking powder and salt.
3. Then, add the butter and mix well.
4. Add the milk, yogurt and maple syrup. Stir until the consistency is smooth and creamy.
5. Sprinkle in the bacon bits.
6. Pour the batter evenly into the pan. Be careful not to fill the pan too full!
7. Bake for 8 minutes. Carefully rotate your pan and cook for an additional 8 minutes with the cake facing the opposite direction in the oven.
8. Remove from the oven and let cool.
9. You can add a glaze from the "Frosting and Glazes" section for a sweeter taste, or eat it without.

HAM AND CHEESE OMELETTE

INGREDIENTS

- ➢ 1 egg
- ➢ ½ tablespoon of milk
- ➢ A tiny pinch of salt
- ➢ 1 tablespoon of shredded cheese
- ➢ 2 tablespoons of small chunks of pre-cooked ham

INSTRUCTIONS

1. Preheat your oven and spray your cooking pan with oil.
2. In a small bowl, whisk together the egg and the milk.
3. Stir the salt, cheese, and ham into the mixture.
4. Pour the mixture into the pan. Follow instructions on your toy oven and cook for 15 minutes. You may want to have an adult help you rotate the pan at about 7 minutes so that it cooks evenly on both sides.
5. When it's finished, you can sprinkle some more cheese on top or just eat it the way it is.

HOMEMADE HASH BROWN CAKES

INGREDIENTS

- ➤ 2 tablespoons of shredded, hash brown potatoes or
- ➤ 2 tablespoons of shredded, yukon gold potatoes
- ➤ Pinch of salt
- ➤ Pinch of pepper
- ➤ 1 tablespoon of shredded parmesan cheese
- ➤ 1 tablespoon of egg, beaten
- ➤ 2 tablespoons of ketchup

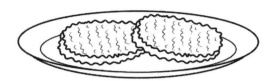

INSTRUCTIONS

1. Preheat your toy oven and spray your cooking pan with oil.
2. If using a freshly peeled potato, make sure you squeeze ALL the juice out before mixing shredded potato in with the rest of the ingredients. If using hashbrowns, make sure they have thawed for a few minutes before using them.
3. In a small bowl, mix the potato, salt, pepper, and egg.
4. Add the parmesan cheese.
5. Pack your mixture together by hand and form 4 small balls or circles, the size of a quarter.
6. Arrange them onto the cooking pan and flatten them until they look like small discs.
7. This part can be tricky, but as long as they are somewhat round, your potato cakes will be fine.
8. Bake your potato cakes for 18 minutes. You may want to have an adult help you rotate the pan after 9 minutes so that your oven can cook them evenly on both sides.
9. Remove from the oven and let them cool a few minutes.
10. Enjoy your hash browns with a side of ketchup.

BAKED PEACH BREAKFAST PARFAIT

INGREDIENTS

- ➤ 4-5 peach slices (fresh or canned)
- ➤ 1 teaspoon of maple syrup
- ➤ 2 teaspoons of brown sugar
- ➤ ⅛ teaspoon of cinnamon
- ➤ 1 tablespoon of granola
- ➤ 2 tablespoons of vanilla yogurt

INSTRUCTIONS

1. Preheat your toy oven and spray your cooking pan with oil.
2. Place your peach slices into a small bowl.
3. Add maple syrup, brown sugar and cinnamon to the peach slices and give it a good stir.
4. Pour the peaches onto the sprayed cooking pan.
5. Follow the instructions on your toy oven and cook for 14 minutes.
6. Remove from the oven and allow the peaches to cool for 2 minutes.
7. Spread the yogurt on top of the peaches.
8. Sprinkle the granola on top of the yogurt and enjoy!

MINI QUICHE (ADVANCED)

INGREDIENTS

- ➢ Refrigerated pie dough (see "Pie Crust" recipe)
- ➢ 1 egg
- ➢ 1 tablespoon of cream
- ➢ A small pinch of salt
- ➢ ½ tablespoon of shredded cheddar cheese
- ➢ ½ tablespoon of bacon bits
- ➢ ½ tablespoon of feta cheese for the top

INSTRUCTIONS

1. Preheat your toy oven and spray your cooking pan with oil.
2. Take a small piece of chilled pie dough, roughly the size of a golf ball.
3. Roll out the pastry dough so that it is nice and thin in the shape of an oval.
4. Carefully transfer the rolled out dough onto the baking pan and place it in the center.
5. Have an adult help you pinch the edges around the dough so that there is space for the filling.
6. Bake for 10 minutes.
7. While the crust is baking, make the filling.
8. In a small bowl, whisk together the egg and the cream.
9. Stir the salt, cheese, and bacon bits into the mixture.
10. Once the crust is finished baking, carefully scoop 2-3 tablespoons of the egg mixture onto the crust.
11. Follow the instructions on your toy oven and cook for 7 minutes.
12. Have an adult help you rotate the pan and place it back in the oven for another 7 minutes so that it cooks evenly on both sides. Be careful, the pan will be hot!
13. Remove the pan and add the feta cheese on top.
14. Allow your quiche to cool a few minutes before eating.

SPICED CHEESE OMELETTE

INGREDIENTS

- ➤ 1 egg
- ➤ ½ tablespoon of milk
- ➤ Small pinch of salt
- ➤ Small pinch of pepper
- ➤ Small pinch of paprika
- ➤ 1 tablespoon of pepper jack cheese

INSTRUCTIONS

1. Preheat your toy oven and spray your cooking pan with oil.
2. In a small bowl, whisk together the egg and the milk.
3. Next add the salt, pepper, and paprika.
4. Add the cheese into the mixture and stir everything together.
5. Carefully pour 4 tablespoons of the egg mixture into the pan.
   Tip: Remember not to fill your pan too full so it doesn't overflow while baking.
6. Follow instructions in your toy oven and cook for 15 minutes. You may want to have an adult help you rotate the pan at about 7 minutes so that it cooks evenly on both sides.

CRANBERRY SCONES FROM SCRATCH

INGREDIENTS

- ➢ 2 tablespoons of plain flour
- ➢ 1 teaspoon of cold butter
- ➢ 2 teaspoons of plain yogurt
- ➢ 2 teaspoons of white sugar
- ➢ ⅛ teaspoon of baking powder
- ➢ ⅛ teaspoon of cream of tartar
- ➢ ½ tablespoon of dried cranberries
- ➢ Premade vanilla Icing

INSTRUCTIONS

1. Preheat your oven and spray your baking sheet with nonstick cooking spray.
2. In a small bowl, mix together the flour, sugar, baking powder, and cream of tartar.
3. Add the butter and yogurt and mix together until a dough forms.
4. You may want to use your hands to pat the dough together.
5. Mix in the cranberries.
6. Shape the dough into a ball, and then flatten it with the end of a spatula.
7. Using a butterknife, cut the dough into fourths so that there are four small triangles.
8. Arrange them on the tray to bake.
9. Make sure they have enough space to bake and are flat enough to fit inside the oven.
10. Cook for 14 minutes.
11. Let them cool a few minutes before eating and drizzle vanilla icing over the top.

BACON CHEDDAR BISCUITS FROM SCRATCH

INGREDIENTS

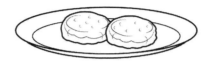

- ➢ 1 ½ tablespoons of plain flour
- ➢ ⅛ teaspoon of baking powder
- ➢ ¼ teaspoon of sugar
- ➢ 1 teaspoon of cold butter
- ➢ 2 teaspoons of milk
- ➢ ½ teaspoon of shredded cheddar cheese
- ➢ ½ teaspoon of cooked bacon bits

INSTRUCTIONS

1. Preheat your toy oven and spray your baking sheet with nonstick cooking spray.
2. In a small bowl, mix together the flour, baking powder, and sugar.
3. Add the butter, milk and cheese and mix with your hands until a dough is formed.
4. Mix in the bacon bits.
5. Roll the dough into tiny little balls and place them on the tray to bake.
6. You should have two rows of three.
   Tip: Make sure they have enough room to bake and are small enough to fit in the oven!
7. Cook for 6 minutes.
8. Have an adult help you carefully rotate your pan and cook for another 6 minutes so that your biscuits cook evenly on both sides.
9. Allow your biscuits a few minutes to cool before eating.

BARBECUE CHICKEN PIZZA FROM SCRATCH

INGREDIENTS

Pizza Dough:

- ➤ 4 tablespoons of plain flour
- ➤ 2 tablespoons of water
- ➤ ⅛ teaspoon of instant yeast
- ➤ A pinch of salt

Pizza Toppings:

- ➤ ½ tablespoon of barbecue sauce
- ➤ 4 teaspoons of grated monterey jack cheese
- ➤ 3 teaspoons of cooked, shredded chicken

INSTRUCTIONS

1. Preheat your toy oven and spray your cooking pan with non-stick cooking oil.
2. First you will make your pizza dough.
3. In a small bowl, mix together the flour, yeast and salt. Add in the water and then knead the dough for 1 minute.
4. Divide the dough in half.
5. Roll or pat the dough into two small balls.
6. Flatten the pizza bases into two small circles and place them beside each other on your cooking pan.
7. Now it's time to add the toppings. Cover the bases of your pizzas with the barbecue sauce. Top with the cheese and cooked chicken.
8. Bake for 14 minutes.
9. Allow your pizzas a few minutes to cool before eating.

CHEESE QUESADILLA

INGREDIENTS

- ➢ 2 small flour tortillas or 1 large flour tortilla
- ➢ 3 teaspoons of grated cheddar cheese
- ➢ 2 teaspoons of your favorite salsa
- ➢ 1 teaspoon of sour cream

INSTRUCTIONS

1. Preheat your toy oven and spray your cooking pan with oil.
2. Use a circular cookie cutter to cut the big tortilla into 2 mini tortillas.
3. Place one onto the pan.
4. Cover the mini tortilla with cheese. Then layer the other tortilla on top so that the cheese is sandwiched in between the two tortillas.
5. Follow your toy oven's instructions and bake for 10 minutes.
6. Serve with salsa and sour cream for some yummy dips.

CHEESY NACHO DIP PRETZELS FROM SCRATCH

INGREDIENTS

- ➤ 4 tablespoons of flour, plus a little extra for rolling out the dough
- ➤ 1/4 teaspoon of baking soda
- ➤ 1/2 tablespoon of white sugar
- ➤ A small pinch of salt
- ➤ 1 tablespoon of butter, room temperature
- ➤ 1 tablespoon of milk
- ➤ 1 tablespoon of shredded cheddar cheese
- ➤ 1-2 tablespoons of Tostitos Nacho Cheese Sauce

INSTRUCTIONS

1. Preheat your oven and spray your cooking pan with non-stick cooking oil.
2. In a small bowl, mix together the flour, baking soda, sugar, and salt.
3. Add the butter and stir until crumbly. Stir in the shredded cheese.
4. Slowly add in the milk while stirring until a mound of dough forms.
5. Divide dough into 4 equal balls of dough.
6. Take one ball of dough and sprinkle it with flour.
7. Using a cutting board, carefully roll dough into a long rope, roughly 11 inches in length.
8. Form a 'U' shape with the dough.
9. Cross the two top ends of the dough so that there is an 'X' at the top. Now flip the X down so that the ends touch the bottom of the U.
10. You should have a traditional pretzel shape.
11. Repeat steps 6-9 until you have four pretzels.
12. Arrange two pretzels on the pan and pop them in the oven for 15 minutes.
13. Enjoy with Tostitos Nacho Cheese for a savory dip.

CORNBREAD FROM SCRATCH

INGREDIENTS

- ➢ 3 ½ teaspoons of fine cornmeal
- ➢ 2 teaspoons of plain flour
- ➢ 1 teaspoon of sugar
- ➢ ⅛ teaspoon of baking powder
- ➢ A small pinch of salt
- ➢ 1 teaspoon of vegetable oil
- ➢ 3 teaspoons of milk
- ➢ 2 teaspoons of applesauce

INSTRUCTIONS

1. Preheat your toy oven and spray your cooking pan with non-stick cooking oil.
2. In a small bowl, mix together the cornmeal, flour, sugar, baking powder and salt.
3. In a separate small mixing bowl, mix together the oil, applesauce and milk.
4. Slowly add the wet mixture to the dry ingredients, one tablespoon at a time.
5. Mix well until fully combined.
6. Pour the batter into the cooking pan.
7. Follow instructions on your toy oven and bake for 14-16 minutes.

CHEESY PESTO STRAWS

INGREDIENTS

➢ Refrigerated pie dough (see "Pie Crust" recipe)
➢ 9 teaspoons of grated cheese
➢ 3 teaspoons of pesto

INSTRUCTIONS

1. Spray cooking pan with non-stick cooking oil.
2. Have an adult help you roll out a piece of dough so that it's nice and thin, and roughly 3x5 inches.
3. Spread the rectangle with pesto sauce, and sprinkle the cheese on top.
4. Get an adult to help you cut the pastry into little strips, about 5-7 rectangles.
5. Twist the rectangles so that they look like a rope and place them on the tray to bake.
6. Follow instructions on your toy oven and bake for 10 minutes. The pesto straws should be a nice golden-brown.

MINI NACHOS

INGREDIENTS

- ➢ Small handful of corn tortilla chips
- ➢ 4 teaspoons of salsa
- ➢ 6 teaspoons of grated cheddar cheese
- ➢ 3 teaspoons of guacamole (optional)

INSTRUCTIONS

1. Preheat your toy oven. Spray cooking pan with non-stick cooking oil.
2. Place 2-3 chips on the cooking pan. You can break them up if you need to so that they will fit in the oven.
3. Cover the chips with the salsa. Then sprinkle the cheese on top of the salsa.
4. Follow instructions on your toy oven and bake for 10 minutes.
5. Serve your nachos with a side of guacamole dip.

MINI THREE CHEESE PIZZA FROM SCRATCH

INGREDIENTS

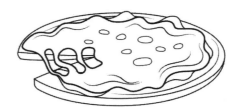

- ➢ 4 tablespoons of plain flour
- ➢ 2 tablespoons of water
- ➢ 1/4 teaspoon of active or instant yeast
- ➢ A pinch of salt
- ➢ 1 jar pizza sauce or marinara sauce
- ➢ 2 teaspoons of grated cheddar cheese
- ➢ 2 teaspoons of grated mozzarella cheese
- ➢ 2 teaspoons of grated monterey jack

INSTRUCTIONS

1. Preheat your oven and spray your cooking pan with non-stick cooking oil.
2. First, you will make your pizza dough. In a small bowl, mix together flour, yeast and salt. Add in the water and then knead the dough for 2 minutes.
3. Roll or pat the dough into two flat discs and arrange them on the pan beside one another. If the dough is too big, you can divide the dough in half before shaping your pizza.
4. Cover the base of your pizza with pizza sauce. Add the cheeses on top.
5. Bake for 10-12 minutes.
6. Allow the pizza a few minutes to cool before enjoying.

PIGGIES WRAPPED IN BLANKETS

INGREDIENTS

➤ 2-3 Hillshire Farm Lit'l Smokies Sausages
➤ ¼ tube of pre-made croissant or biscuit dough
➤ Mustard or ketchup for dipping

INSTRUCTIONS

1. Preheat your oven and spray your cooking pan with non-stick cooking oil.
2. Roll out the dough until it's almost as thin as a quarter
3. Cut it into tiny little rectangles about 2 inches long and half an inch wide.
4. Slice the sausages into small, round pieces.
5. Wrap just enough dough to fit around the sausage and leave a little bit of the sausage poking out of the dough.
6. Repeat until all your piggies are wrapped in their blankets.
7. Add a few to the pan. You may have to squish them on top a bit so that they will fit in the oven.
8. Bake for 7 minutes.
9. Have an adult help you rotate your pan and bake them on the other side for another 7 minutes. Careful, the pan will be hot!
10. Then remove them from the oven and let them cool a few minutes before eating. You can serve them with a side of ketchup or mustard as a dipping sauce.

CLASSIC SALTED PRETZELS

INGREDIENTS

Pretzels:

- ➤ 4 tablespoons of flour, plus a little extra for rolling out the dough
- ➤ 1/4 teaspoon of baking soda
- ➤ 1/2 tablespoon of white sugar
- ➤ A small pinch of salt
- ➤ 1 tablespoon of butter, room temperature
- ➤ 1 tablespoon of milk

Topping:

- ➤ 1 tablespoon of melted butter
- ➤ 1 teaspoon of coarse sea salt

INSTRUCTIONS

1. Preheat your oven and spray your cooking pan with non-stick cooking oil.
2. In a small bowl, mix together flour, baking soda, sugar, and salt.
3. Add the butter and stir until crumbly.
4. Slowly add in the milk while stirring until a mound of dough forms.
5. Divide dough into 4 equal sized balls of dough.
6. Take one ball of dough and sprinkle it with flour.
7. Using a cutting board, carefully roll dough into a long rope, roughly 11 inches.
8. Make a 'U' shape with the dough. Cross the two top ends of the dough so that there is an 'X' at the top. Now flip the X down so that the ends touch the bottom of the U.
9. You should have a traditional pretzel shape.
10. Repeat steps 6-9 until you have four pretzels.
11. Now it's time to make the topping. Have an adult help you melt 1 tablespoon of butter in the microwave.
12. Sprinkle the pretzels with salt and brush with melted butter.
13. Arrange two pretzels in the pan and pop them in the toy oven for 15 minutes.

CINNAMON SUGAR RAISIN PRETZELS

INGREDIENTS

Pretzels:

- ➢ 4 tablespoons of flour, plus a little extra for rolling out the dough
- ➢ 1/4 teaspoon of baking soda
- ➢ 1/2 tablespoon of white sugar
- ➢ A small pinch of salt
- ➢ 1 tablespoon of butter, room temperature
- ➢ 1 tablespoon of milk
- ➢ ½ teaspoon of cinnamon
- ➢ 2 teaspoons of raisins

Cinnamon Sugar Topping:

- ➢ 1 tablespoon of brown sugar
- ➢ 1 teaspoon of cinnamon
- ➢ 1/2 tablespoon of soft butter

INSTRUCTIONS

1. Preheat your oven and spray your cooking pan with non-stick cooking oil.
2. In a small bowl, mix together the flour, baking soda, sugar, and salt.
   Add the butter and stir until crumbly.
3. Stir in the raisins and cinnamon.
4. Slowly add in the milk and mix until a mound of dough forms. Divide dough into 4 equal balls.
5. Take one ball of dough and sprinkle it with flour.
6. Using a cutting board, carefully roll the dough into a long rope, roughly 11 inches long.
7. Shape your pretzels by making a 'U' shape with the dough, then cross the two ends of the dough so that there is an 'X' at the top.
8. Flip the X down so that the ends touch the bottom of the U. You should have a traditional pretzel shape.
9. Repeat steps 5-8 until you have four pretzels.
10. Arrange two pretzels on the pan and pop them in the oven for 14 minutes.
11. While they are baking, make the cinnamon sugar topping. Stir together brown sugar, cinnamon, and butter in a bowl.
12. Carefully place the pretzels in the bowl and coat them with the sweet topping, then set them on a plate. Allow them to cool a few moments before enjoying your sweet treat.

CHEESY POTATO CASSEROLE

INGREDIENTS

- ➤ 3 tablespoons of pre-cut hash browns
- ➤ 1 tablespoon of grated cheese
- ➤ 1 teaspoon of cooked bacon bits
- ➤ 2 teaspoons of sour cream
- ➤ 1 pinch of pepper
- ➤ 1 pinch of salt

INSTRUCTIONS

1. Preheat your toy oven and spray your cooking pan with non-stick cooking oil.
2. In a small bowl, combine hash browns, cheese, bacon bits, salt, pepper and sour cream.
3. Mix everything together with a spoon.
4. Pour the hashbrowns evenly onto the sprayed cooking pan.
5. Follow your toy oven's instructions and bake for 15-17 minutes.

CHEESE WHEELS

INGREDIENTS

➢ Refrigerated puff pastry dough or pie dough (see "Pie Crust" recipe)

➢ 2 tablespoons of grated cheese

INSTRUCTIONS

1. Preheat your toy oven and spray your cooking pan with oil.
2. Break off a piece of pastry dough that's roughly the size of a golf ball.
3. Roll and pat your dough into a small rectangle.
4. Next, continue to roll and pat the rectangle until it's almost as thin as a coin.
5. Cover the rectangle with grated cheese.
6. Roll the rectangle into a log, by starting from one end of the rectangle and rolling it up to the other end. Be careful not to let too much cheese spill out!
7. Slice the pastry into little cheese wheels, no more than half an inch thick.
8. Arrange your cheese wheels on the tray to bake.
9. Bake for 10-13 minutes.
10. For more evenly baked pastry wheels, rotate your pan after 5 minutes so that the pastries cook well on both sides.
11. Remove from the oven and let cool before eating.

QUICK CORNBREAD FROM MUFFIN MIX

This recipe works well with Jiffy's cornbread muffin mix, but you can also try it with another blend. Just keep in mind that the consistency might be slightly different.

INGREDIENTS

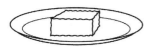

- ➢ 2 tablespoons of Jiffy cornbread mix
- ➢ 1 tablespoon of applesauce
- ➢ 1 tablespoon of milk
- ➢ ½ teaspoon of room temperature butter

INSTRUCTIONS

1. Preheat your oven and spray your baking sheet with nonstick cooking spray.
2. In a small bowl, combine cornbread mix, applesauce, milk, and butter.
3. Mix everything together.
4. Pour into pan and spread evenly.
5. Follow directions on your toy oven and cook for 9 minutes.
6. Carefully remove the pan and place it back in the oven facing the opposite direction for another 9 minutes.
7. Remove from oven. Allow your pan to cool a few minutes before enjoying your cornbread.

ST. PATTY'S DAY RICE CRISPY TREATS

INGREDIENTS

- 1 ½ teaspoons of butter
- 3 tablespoons of marshmallow creme
- ½ teaspoon of white sugar
- 4-5 tablespoons of rice crisp cereal
- 1 drop of green food coloring
- A spoonful of Lucky Charm marshmallows (optional)

INSTRUCTIONS

1. Preheat your toy oven and spray your cooking pan with oil.
2. Spoon butter and marshmallow creme onto the greased cooking pan.
3. Have an adult help you cover the baking sheet with a piece of foil and secure it over the top of the marshmallow mixture.
   WARNING: Do not skip this step. It's important to completely cover your pan so that the marshmallow mixture doesn't come out in your oven.
4. Follow your toy oven's cooking instructions and place the baking sheet in the oven for 8 minutes.
5. Have an adult help you transfer the marshmallow mixture from the baking sheet into a bowl. Careful —it might be hot!
6. Add a drop of green food coloring and the puffed rice cereal into the bowl with the warmed marshmallow mixture and stir everything together.
7. Scoop the mixture out of the bowl and press it back into the cookie sheet until it's evenly spread across the pan. Sprinkle your Lucky Charms on top.
8. Place your rice crispy treats in the fridge for approximately 5-10 minutes to harden a bit before you eat them.

VALENTINE'S SUGAR COOKIES FROM SCRATCH

INGREDIENTS

- 2 teaspoons of butter
- 3 teaspoons of sugar
- 2 drops of vanilla extract
- 1 teaspoon of applesauce
- 2 ½ tablespoons of flour
- ⅛ teaspoon of baking soda
- 2 tablespoons of powdered sugar
- ½ teaspoon of water
- A drop of red food coloring
- Pink sprinkles
- Mini heart shaped cookie cutters

INSTRUCTIONS

1. Preheat your oven and spray your baking sheet with nonstick cooking spray.
2. Mix together the butter and sugar in a small bowl, until light and fluffy.
3. Add the vanilla and applesauce to the butter mixture.
4. Sprinkle in the flour and baking soda. Stir everything together. The batter should thicken and form a dough. You may need to use your hands a bit to help.
5. Roll the dough out so that it's nice and thin.
6. Cut the dough into mini heart shaped cookies.
7. Arrange two cookies on your sprayed cookie sheet. Make sure they have enough room to bake and are small enough to fit in your toy oven!
8. Bake for 8-10 minutes.
9. Once the cookies have cooled, you can decorate them.
10. Make the icing by mixing together the powdered sugar, water and food coloring.
11. Spread the icing on top of the cookies, then add some sprinkles to each one. Leave to dry before eating.

RED HOT BROWNIES

INGREDIENTS

Brownies

- ➤ 1 ½ tablespoons of plain flour
- ➤ 2 teaspoons of oil
- ➤ 2 teaspoons of cocoa powder
- ➤ 1 tablespoon of white sugar
- ➤ ⅛ teaspoon baking powder
- ➤ 1-2 drops of vanilla extract
- ➤ A small pinch of salt
- ➤ 1 tablespoon of milk
- ➤ 1 teaspoon of applesauce

Glaze

- ➤ 1 tablespoon of butter
- ➤ 2 tablespoons of powdered sugar
- ➤ ¼ teaspoon of cinnamon
- ➤ 1-2 drops of red food coloring
- ➤ ¼ teaspoon of milk
- ➤ 1 teaspoon of Red Hots Cinnamon Flavored Candy

INSTRUCTIONS

1. Preheat your toy oven and spray your cooking pan with oil.
2. First, make the brownies by combining all the brownie ingredients into a small bowl.
3. Mix everything together until your batter is smooth.
4. Pour your brownie batter into your greased cooking pan.
5. Bake for 7 minutes. Remove your pan, rotate it, and place it back in the oven for another 7 minutes so it cooks evenly on both sides.
6. While your brownies are cooking, make the glaze.
7. In a small bowl, mix butter, cinnamon, and powdered sugar together.
8. Add the milk and food coloring. Stir until there are no more clumps of butter.
9. Set the glaze in the fridge while the brownies are cooling.
10. When your brownies have cooled completely, spread the glaze on top for a pretty, pink finish. Sprinkle the Red Hots on top.

EASTER BIRD'S NEST COOKIES

INGREDIENTS

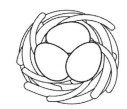

- ➢ 1 tablespoon of butterscotch chips
- ➢ 1 tablespoon of milk chocolate chips
- ➢ 1 teaspoon of peanut butter
- ➢ 3 tablespoons of crispy chow mein noodles
- ➢ A small handful of mini Cadbury Milk Chocolate Eggs

INSTRUCTIONS

1. Preheat your toy oven and spray your cooking pan with non-stick cooking oil.
2. Make sure it's greased so that the cookies don't stick.
3. In a small microwavable bowl, add the milk chocolate chips, butterscotch chips, and peanut butter.
4. Have an adult help you warm the bowl in the microwave for 60 seconds.
5. Stir the contents until it looks smooth and creamy.
6. Add the chow mein noodles and stir everything together.
7. Scoop out a small spoon full of batter and place it on one side of the tray.
8. Repeat on the other side so that you have two small nests beside each other. Tip: You may need to rearrange a few noodles so that they fit inside the oven's opening.
9. Follow the instructions on your toy oven and bake for 6 minutes.
10. When it's finished baking, arrange 3 mini Cadbury Chocolate Eggs on each cookie.
11. Carefully place your pan of cookies in the freezer for 5 minutes so the cookies can harden.
12. When they've finished setting, have an adult help you use a soft spatula to check if they're done and gently lift them off the tray. Enjoy!

CHRISTMAS GINGERBREAD COOKIES (ADVANCED)

INGREDIENTS

- ➢ 2 tablespoons of plain flour
- ➢ 2 teaspoons of butter
- ➢ 2 teaspoons of brown sugar
- ➢ 2 teaspoons of dark molasses
- ➢ ¼ teaspoon of vanilla extract
- ➢ 1 teaspoon of applesauce
- ➢ ⅛ teaspoon of baking soda
- ➢ ¼ teaspoon of ginger
- ➢ ½ teaspoon of allspice
- ➢ Mini christmas cookie cutters (optional)

INSTRUCTIONS

Tip: It can help to use wax or parchment paper when rolling out this dough. Place the cookie dough in between the paper and use a rolling pin on top of the paper. Always remember to remove the paper prior to baking. Wax and parchment paper should never go inside your toy oven.

1. Preheat your toy oven and spray your cooking pan with oil.
2. Add the butter to a small bowl and microwave for 20 seconds.
3. Next, add the sugar, molasses and vanilla to the butter. Stir everything together.
4. In a separate bowl, combine flour, baking soda, ginger, nutmeg and cinnamon. Stir everything together.
5. Add the molasses mixture to the bowl with flour and mix everything together until dough forms. Set it in the freezer for 7 minutes.
6. Roll out the gingerbread so that it's nice and thin, like a flat coin. You can sprinkle some extra flour on it if you need to.
7. For your cookies, you can use mini Christmas cookie cutters or shape them yourself.
8. Arrange your gingerbread shapes onto the pan and bake for 8-10 minutes.
9. When you're ready to decorate your cookies, you can choose a recipe from the "Frostings and Glazes" section.

PUMPKIN SPICE COOKIES

INGREDIENTS

- ➢ 1 ½ teaspoons of canned pumpkin puree
- ➢ 2 tablespoons of flour
- ➢ ⅛ teaspoon of baking soda
- ➢ 2 teaspoons of sugar
- ➢ 2 teaspoons of milk
- ➢ 2 drops of vanilla extract
- ➢ ⅛ teaspoon of cinnamon
- ➢ ⅛ teaspoon of ground nutmeg

INSTRUCTIONS

1. Preheat your toy oven and spray your cooking sheet with nonstick cooking spray.
2. Mix flour, baking soda, sugar, cinnamon and nutmeg together in a bowl.
3. Add the pumpkin puree and vanilla extract and mix with a small spoon. Slowly add the milk while stirring. The mix should thicken like cookie dough. You may need to use your hands a bit for this part.
4. Scoop out a marble size amount and place it on your sprayed cooking sheet. Make sure they have enough room to bake and are small enough to fit in the oven.
5. Repeat this until there are six balls of cookie dough total.
6. Follow your toy oven's cooking instructions and cook for 8 minutes.
7. Rotate your pan and put them back in the oven for another 8 minutes.
8. Remove from the oven and let the cookies cool a few minutes before eating.

HOLIDAY TREE COOKIES

INGREDIENTS

- 2 teaspoons of butter
- 2 teaspoons of sugar
- 2 drops of vanilla extract
- 1 teaspoon of applesauce
- 2 ½ teaspoons of flour
- ⅛ teaspoon of baking powder
- 2 tablespoons of powdered sugar
- ½ teaspoon of milk
- A few drops of green food coloring
- Gold and silver sprinkles
- Circle or tree cookie cutters

INSTRUCTIONS

1. Preheat your toy oven and spray your pan with cooking spray.
2. Mix together the butter and sugar in a small bowl.
3. Add the vanilla, food coloring and applesauce to the bowl and stir.
4. Stir in the flour and baking powder. Stir everything together and the mix should thicken like cookie dough. You may need to use your hands a bit for this part.
5. Roll the dough out so that it's nice and thin.
6. Using your cookie cutters, cut the dough into 4-6 tree shapes.
7. Place the cookies on the tray to bake. Make sure they have enough room to bake and are small enough to fit in the oven!
8. Bake for 5 minutes, then rotate your pan and bake for another 5 minutes with the pan facing the opposite direction.
9. Once the cookies have cooled, you can decorate them.
10. Make the icing by mixing together the powdered sugar, and milk.
11. Drizzle the icing on top of each cookie and add the gold or silver sprinkles. Let your cookies dry before eating.

JACK-O'- LANTERN COOKIES

INGREDIENTS

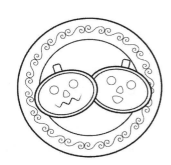

- ➢ Refrigerated sugar cookie dough (You may use store bought or make your own by using the "Sugar Cookie" recipe in this book)
- ➢ Prepared orange "Cookie Icing" (recipe included in this book)
- ➢ Black icing pen
- ➢ 4-5 pieces of Brach's Mini Candy Corn
- ➢ Chocolate chips

INSTRUCTIONS

1. Spray your cooking pan with non-stick cooking oil.
2. Get an adult to help you roll and pat your sugar cookie dough into two little ovals.
3. Add a stem to the top of your pumpkin by shaping tiny squares and attaching them to the top of your oval for a pumpkin stem.
4. Arrange two cookies on the cooking pan. Follow the instructions on your toy oven and bake for 8 minutes.
5. While your cookies are baking, make the icing.
6. Once your cookies have cooled, you can decorate them to look like faces on a pumpkin.
7. Cover the top of the cookie with orange icing.
8. Add a candy corn in the center of the oval for the nose, and two chocolate chips for the eyes on top.
9. Last, draw a zigzag line with your icing pen, just below the nose. You can also get creative and make your own spooky faces.

VANILLA SHORTBREAD COOKIES

INGREDIENTS

- ➤ 2 tablespoons of plain flour
- ➤ 4 teaspoons of cold butter
- ➤ 3 teaspoons of white sugar
- ➤ ½ teaspoon of vegetable oil
- ➤ 2-3 drops of vanilla extract

INSTRUCTIONS

1. Preheat your toy oven and spray your cooking pan with oil.
2. Rub the butter and flour together until they begin to look like fine breadcrumbs.
3. Add the sugar, oil and vanilla.
4. Roll or press the ingredients together until it forms a dough. If your shortbread cookie dough is too soft, place it in the fridge to harden for 5 minutes before shaping your cookies.
5. Press your shortbread cookie dough into tiny rectangles or circles onto the pan. You might need to get an adult to help you shape them.
6. Make sure your cookies are flat enough to fit inside the oven's opening. If you need to, press on their tops with a flat spatula or fork.
7. Bake for 7 minutes.
8. Carefully remove your pan from the oven and rotate the pan so that it finishes baking on the other side for another 7 minutes.
9. Remove from the oven and let cool before eating.

CORNFLAKE WREATHS

INGREDIENTS

- ➢ 1 ½ teaspoon of butter
- ➢ 2 tablespoons of marshmallow creme
- ➢ ¼ teaspoon of vanilla
- ➢ 4 tablespoons of broken corn flake cereal
- ➢ 1-2 drops of green food coloring
- ➢ Red Hot Cinnamon Candies

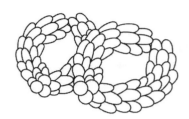

INSTRUCTIONS

1. Preheat your toy oven and spray your cooking pan with oil.
2. Have an adult help you crush your cornflakes so that they are in smaller pieces. Tip: they don't have to be completely crushed into powder, but it helps if they are broken up a little so that they fit inside your toy oven.
3. Heat the butter and marshmallow creme in the microwave for about 30 seconds and stir. Repeat until the contents are creamy.
4. Have an adult help you transfer the marshmallow mixture from the baking sheet and into a bowl. Careful—it might be hot!
5. Add the green food coloring and vanilla and stir.
6. Add the cornflake cereal last, and mix it all together.
7. Use your hands to scoop the mixture out of the bowl and shape two little hollow circles on your greased cookie sheet.
8. You can decorate your wreaths with Red Hot Candies to make it look more like a Christmas wreath.
9. Bake for 6 minutes. Then remove your pan from the oven and place them in the fridge to harden for 10 minutes before eating.

CINNAMON ROLLS (ADVANCED)

INGREDIENTS

The Rolls:
- ➢ 3 ½ tablespoons of flour, plus 1 tablespoon for rolling
- ➢ 1 tablespoon of white sugar
- ➢ A small pinch of salt
- ➢ ½ tablespoon of butter
- ➢ 1 tablespoon of milk
- ➢ ¼ teaspoon of instant yeast
- ➢ 1 teaspoon of applesauce

The Filling:
- ➢ ½ tablespoon of butter
- ➢ 1 tablespoon of brown sugar
- ➢ 1 teaspoon of cinnamon

INSTRUCTIONS

1. Preheat your toy oven and spray your cooking pan with oil.
2. In a small microwavable bowl, combine milk and butter. Have an adult help you microwave the bowl's contents for 25 seconds.
3. Sprinkle the yeast into the milk and butter mixture. Set aside.
4. In a separate bowl, mix flour, white sugar, and salt.
5. Add the applesauce.
6. Next, combine the milk and butter mixture with the flour mixture.
7. Stir everything together until a dough begins to form and knead for 1-2 minutes.
8. Set dough aside while you make the filling. Combine the butter, brown sugar and cinnamon in a small bowl. Mix everything together.
9. Sprinkle some flour onto a large cutting board and roll out your dough into a big, flat rectangle. It should be approximately 3x7 inches.
10. Spread the sugar filling onto the dough.
11. Have an adult help you fold the dough into a tight roll.
12. Once it's rolled into a big log, slice the dough into about ¼ or ½ inch rolls.
13. There should be roughly 10-12 rolls when you've finished.
14. Arrange them on the tray to bake. You may need to flatten them a bit so that they fit inside the oven's opening.
15. Bake your rolls for 10 minutes. Then flip the tray around and bake them for another 8 minutes. Remove from the oven and allow them to cool before eating.

CHOCOLATE FUDGE BROWNIES

INGREDIENTS

- ➢ 2 tablespoons of all-purpose flour
- ➢ 2 teaspoons of cocoa powder
- ➢ ¼ teaspoon of baking powder
- ➢ 1 tiny pinch of salt
- ➢ 1 ½ teaspoons of butter (softened)
- ➢ 1 tablespoon of white sugar
- ➢ 1 tablespoon of milk
- ➢ ½ tablespoon of chocolate chips

INSTRUCTIONS

1. Preheat your oven and spray your cooking pan with nonstick cooking oil.
2. Add the flour, cocoa powder, baking powder and salt to a bowl. Stir everything together with a small spatula.
3. Next, add the butter and white sugar and mix everything together until the batter forms a gritty texture. You might need to use your hands to help mix everything together.
4. Last, add the milk and stir until a batter forms.
5. Carefully spoon the brownie batter onto the greased cooking pan, leaving a little space on top for the chocolate chips.
6. Sprinkle the chocolate chips on top of the batter.
7. Bake brownies for 7 minutes.
8. Rotate your pan and bake for another 7 minutes so that the brownies can cook evenly on both sides.
9. Remove from the oven and let cool completely before eating. You can eat them by themselves or enjoy with ice cream for a fancy à la mode treat!

BUTTERSCOTCH BLONDIES

INGREDIENTS

- ➤ 2 tablespoons of plain flour
- ➤ ⅛ teaspoon of baking powder
- ➤ 1 tablespoon of butter
- ➤ 1/2 tablespoon of brown sugar
- ➤ 1 tablespoon of white sugar
- ➤ ½ teaspoon of vanilla
- ➤ 1 teaspoon of applesauce
- ➤ 1 tablespoon of butterscotch chips

INSTRUCTIONS

1. Preheat your oven and spray your cooking pan with nonstick cooking oil.
2. In a small bowl, add the flour and baking powder and mix well.
3. Next, add the butter, brown and white sugars, apple sauce, and vanilla.
4. Mix everything together with a spoon.
5. Stir the butterscotch chips into the batter.
6. Spread the batter evenly across the baking sheet.
7. Bake for 13 minutes.
8. Remove from the oven and allow the tray to cool a few minutes before eating.

PIE CRUST

INGREDIENTS

- ➤ 3 tablespoons of flour
- ➤ ½ teaspoon of white sugar
- ➤ ⅛ teaspoon of salt
- ➤ ½ teaspoon of cold, refrigerated butter
- ➤ 1 teaspoon of cold water
- ➤ 2-3 ice cubes

INSTRUCTIONS

1. Preheat your toy oven and spray your cooking pan with cooking oil.
2. Place the ice cubes into a cup with water.
3. In a small bowl, mix the flour, sugar and salt together.
4. Add the butter and mix together until the recipe resembles something similar to gritty sand.
5. Add 1 teaspoon of ice cold water to the bowl and mix together until it forms a dough. You may want to use your hands for this step to help press it together.
6. If using your dough right away, let it chill in the fridge for a few minutes prior to rolling it out into a crust.
7. If you would like to save your pie crust for another recipe, place it in a ziplock bag and leave it in the fridge for up to 4 days.

COOKIE PIZZA

INGREDIENTS

- ➤ 1 ½ teaspoons of butter
- ➤ 2 tablespoons of flour
- ➤ ⅛ teaspoon of baking soda
- ➤ 3 teaspoons of sugar
- ➤ ½ teaspoon of milk
- ➤ 1-2 drops of vanilla extract
- ➤ 1 tablespoon of chocolate chips
- ➤ 3 teaspoons of nutella
- ➤ 2 teaspoons of rainbow sprinkles

INSTRUCTIONS

1. Preheat your oven and spray your cooking pan with non-stick cooking oil.
2. Mix flour, baking soda, and sugar together in a bowl.
3. Add the butter and mix.
4. Slowly add the vanilla extract and milk while forming the dough with your fingers. The mix should thicken like cookie dough.
5. Add the chocolate chips last.
6. Scoop the cookie batter and press it down into one big circle or square on the cooking sheet.
7. Follow directions on your toy oven and cook for 13 minutes.
8. Once the cookie has cooled, you can decorate it.
9. Spread the top of the cookie with nutella, then cover it with rainbow sprinkles.

MINT CHIP BROWNIES (ADVANCED)

INGREDIENTS

- 2 tablespoons of flour
- ⅛ teaspoon of baking powder
- ⅛ teaspoon of salt
- 1 ½ teaspoons of butter
- ½ tablespoon of milk
- 1 teaspoon of sugar
- ½ tablespoon of melted Hershey's Milk Chocolate
- ¼ teaspoon of pure mint extract
- 1 ½ teaspoons of applesauce

Mint Frosting

- 1 tablespoon of butter
- 2 tablespoons of powdered sugar
- ½ teaspoon of milk
- 1-2 drops of green food coloring
- 1 drop of pure mint extract
- 1 tablespoon of crumpled Hershey's Milk Chocolate bar

INSTRUCTIONS

1. Preheat your oven and spray your cooking pan with nonstick cooking oil.
2. Have an adult help you melt 1 tablespoon of Hershey's Milk Chocolate in a small bowl.
3. Add the butter and peppermint to the bowl and stir.
4. Add the flour, baking powder, salt, applesauce, and milk.
5. Mix everything together until your brownie batter forms.
6. Pour the batter evenly into the sprayed cooking pan.
7. Bake for 6 minutes. Then carefully rotate your pan and bake it for another 6 minutes so that it cooks evenly on both sides.
8. While the brownies are cooking, make your mint frosting.
9. In a small bowl, mix together butter, powdered sugar, green food coloring, mint and milk.
10. Stir everything together until a creamy green frosting forms and there are no lumps.
11. Once your brownies have finished baking, remove them from the oven and let them cool a few minutes before adding your mint topping.
12. After you spread the mint frosting over the brownies, sprinkle the crumpled Hershey's bar on top. Enjoy!

PEANUT BUTTER BROWNIES

INGREDIENTS

- ➢ 2 tablespoons of butter
- ➢ ¼ cup of brown sugar
- ➢ ¼ cup of flour
- ➢ ⅓ teaspoon of baking powder
- ➢ ½ teaspoon of vanilla
- ➢ 1 tablespoon of peanut butter
- ➢ 3 tablespoons of mini peanut butter or butterscotch chips

INSTRUCTIONS

1. Preheat the oven and spray your pan with non-stick cooking oil.
2. In a small bowl, mix butter and brown sugar together until creamy.
3. In a separate bowl combine flour and baking powder and stir well. Slowly combine the butter and sugar mixture to the bowl with flour and baking powder.
4. Add vanilla and peanut butter and mix well.
5. Stir mini peanut butter or butterscotch chips into batter. Make sure to save a few for the top!
6. Follow the cooking instructions on your toy oven and cook for 15 minutes.

BLUEBERRY CRUMBLE

INGREDIENTS

The Topping:

- 1 ½ tablespoons of flour
- 3 teaspoons of brown sugar
- 1 tablespoon of plain instant oats
- 1 tablespoon of butter

The Filling:

- 2-3 tablespoons of blueberries
- 1 tablespoon of white sugar
- 1 teaspoon of flour
- ¼ teaspoon of cinnamon
- ¼ teaspoon of vanilla extract
- ½ teaspoon of vegetable oil

INSTRUCTIONS

1. Preheat your oven and spray your cooking pan with oil.
2. Mix together the blueberries, sugar, flour, cinnamon and vanilla in a bowl.
3. Add the blueberry mixture to your pan.
4. In a separate bowl, mix flour, oats, brown sugar and butter until a crumbly topping forms.
5. Sprinkle the crumble mixture on top of the blueberries.
6. Bake for 12-14 minutes and let cool before eating.

APPLE PIE PASTRY

INGREDIENTS

- ➤ Pastry puff dough or pie dough (from the "Pie Crust" recipe)
- ➤ 3 tablespoons of diced apple
- ➤ 3 teaspoons of brown sugar
- ➤ ½ teaspoon of flour
- ➤ ¼ teaspoon of cinnamon
- ➤ ¼ teaspoon of vegetable oil

INSTRUCTIONS

1. Preheat your toy oven and spray your cooking pan with oil.
2. Have an adult help you remove the apple's peeling and core, and dice the apple up into little pieces.
3. Mix together the apple, sugar, oil, flour and cinnamon in a bowl.
4. Add the apple mixture to your pan.
5. Break off a golf ball size of refrigerated pastry or pie dough.
6. Roll the dough out until it's as thin as a quarter.
7. Layer the pastry on top of the pan, so that it covers the apples.
8. Trim off any extra dough so that it fits your pan perfectly.
9. Poke the pastry on top with a fork, so that the air can escape.
10. Bake for 9 minutes.
11. Then remove your pan and place it back in the oven so that it faces the opposite direction. Be sure to use a pot holder so you don't get burned!
12. Bake for another 9 minutes so that it cooks evenly on both sides, or until it's golden brown.
13. Remove the pan from the oven and allow your treat to cool a few minutes before eating.

STRAWBERRY SHORTCAKE

INGREDIENTS

- ➢ 2 tablespoons of flour
- ➢ 1 tablespoon of white sugar
- ➢ ¼ teaspoon of baking powder
- ➢ 3 teaspoons of cold butter
- ➢ 1 tablespoon of milk
- ➢ 1/4 teaspoon of vanilla extract
- ➢ 1 tablespoon of applesauce
- ➢ 3-4 strawberries, washed and sliced into little pieces
- ➢ Whipped cream for the topping

INSTRUCTIONS

1. Preheat your toy oven and spray your baking pan with nonstick cooking oil.
2. In a small bowl, mix together flour, sugar, baking powder and salt.
3. Then, add the butter and mix until the contents resemble a gritty, sand texture. You may want to use your hands to make sure it's mixed together.
4. Add the vanilla and applesauce. Slowly add in the milk and stir until the consistency is smooth and creamy.
5. Pour the batter evenly into your baking sheet. Be careful not to fill the pan too full!
6. Bake for a total of 16 minutes. For a more evenly cooked cake, rotate your cake after 8 minutes so that it bakes evenly on both sides.
7. Once your cake has finished baking, remove from the oven and let cool.
8. Finish by adding sliced strawberries and whipped cream topping to your cake.

PEANUT BUTTER FUDGE (ADVANCED)

INGREDIENTS

- ➤ 1 tablespoon of brown sugar
- ➤ 2 tablespoons of white sugar
- ➤ 1 tablespoon of room temperature butter
- ➤ ¼ teaspoon of vanilla extract
- ➤ 1 tablespoon of marshmallow creme
- ➤ ½ tablespoon of evaporated milk
- ➤ 1 ½ tablespoons of creamy peanut butter

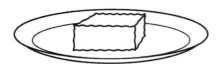

INSTRUCTIONS

1. Preheat your toy oven and spray your cooking pan with nonstick cooking oil.
2. Mix together the butter, brown sugar, white sugar, and vanilla in a small bowl.
3. Stir in the evaporated milk.
4. Pour contents onto the greased cooking pan.
5. Bake for 5 minutes and remove the pan from the oven.
6. Carefully rotate the pan by placing back in the oven so that it faces the opposite direction and bakes for another 5 minutes. This way the contents cook evenly on both sides.
7. Have an adult help you remove the pan from the oven. Be careful to use a pot holder. The pan and its contents will be hot!
8. Have an adult help you transfer the ingredients from the hot pan into a small bowl.
9. While the ingredients are still hot, add the marshmallow creme, vanilla and peanut butter into the bowl and stir everything together until smooth.
10. Spread the batter evenly onto the tray and place in freezer to harden for 5-8 minutes.
11. When it's finished setting, cut your fudge into little squares and enjoy!

CHOCOLATE-MARSHMALLOW WHOOPIE PIES (ADVANCED)

INGREDIENTS

Whoopie Pie Cookies:

- ➤ 2 tablespoons of white sugar
- ➤ 2 teaspoons of butter
- ➤ ¼ teaspoon of vanilla extract
- ➤ 4 teaspoons of flour
- ➤ 2 teaspoons of cocoa powder
- ➤ 1/4 teaspoon of baking powder
- ➤ 2 teaspoons of chocolate chips

Whoopie Pie Filling:

- ➤ 2 teaspoons of marshmallow creme fluff
- ➤ 2 teaspoons of cold butter
- ➤ 2 tablespoons of powdered sugar

INSTRUCTIONS

1. Preheat your oven and spray your cooking pan with non-stick cooking oil.
2. First, you'll make the mini cake shells. Get an adult to help you melt the chocolate chips in the microwave for 30 seconds. Stir the contents together.
3. In the same bowl, add the butter, white sugar, vanilla and stir everything together with the butter and melted chocolate chips.
4. Then, add the flour, cocoa powder, baking powder and hot water.
5. Mix everything together so that the consistency has no more clumps.
6. Scoop the batter onto your sprayed cooking pan into six little circles, roughly the size of quarters.
7. Bake for 7 minutes. Then remove the pan and place it back in the oven for another 7 minutes so that your whoopie pies cook well on both sides. Be careful, the pan will be hot!
8. Set the pan aside to cool while you mix up the filling
9. Mix together the marshmallow creme fluff and butter. Then stir in the powdered sugar and mix until you have a creamy filling.
10. Once the cakes have cooled, spoon a little drop of the filling onto the flat side of one of the cakes. Then stick another cake on top of the spread.
11. Repeat to make a total of three whoopie pies.

ICE CREAM COOKIE SANDWICH (ADVANCED)

INGREDIENTS

- ➤ Refrigerated cookie dough
  (choose from any flavor under "Cookies" recipes)
- ➤ 4-6 tablespoons of ice cream

INSTRUCTIONS

1. Preheat your oven and spray your cooking pan with nonstick cooking oil.
2. Check your cookie recipe's directions for baking.
3. Roll the dough into 4 equal sized balls of dough.
4. If you want bigger cookie sandwiches, make them a bit larger.
5. They should all be the same size and be able to fit onto your pan.
6. Flatten the cookies with the flat side of a spatula so that you have fou, flat circles.
7. Bake your cookies for 6 minutes.
8. Remove your pan and place it back in the oven so that the pan faces the other direction. Let the cookies cook on this side for another 6 minutes.
9. Remove from the oven and let cool for 10 minutes or until no longer warm.
   Tip: you can set your pan in the fridge so that they cool quicker.
10. Once cookies have completely cooled, carefully remove them from the pan and scoop a small spoonful of ice cream onto the flat side of a cookie.
11. Place another cookie on top so that you have a cookie sandwich.
12. You can eat them now, or place them in the freezer for a few minutes if they need to harden before eating.

MINI CAKE POPS (ADVANCED)

INGREDIENTS

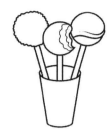

➢ One mini cake fully cooked and cooled
   (choose a box cake or from scratch recipe in this book)
➢ 3 tablespoons of white chocolate chips
➢ 2 teaspoons of butter
➢ Refrigerated "Vanilla Buttercream Frosting"
   (recipe included in this book)
➢ 5-7 toothpicks or lollipop sticks (cut in half)
➢ 1 tablespoon of sprinkles
➢ A drop of food coloring (optional)

INSTRUCTIONS

1. Dump the cake into a small bowl and break it up with a fork so that it's crumbly.
2. Add two teaspoons of vanilla buttercream frosting to the crumbled cake and mix together.
3. Shape the cake into little 1 inch balls and poke a toothpick in the center of each ball.
4. Set inside the freezer to harden for 5-10 minutes.
5. Have an adult help you microwave the white chocolate chips and butter for 30 seconds or until melted.
6. Add the food coloring and stir the melted chocolate and butter until creamy.
7. Add the sprinkles.
8. Holding the ends of your toothpick, carefully dip the cake pops in the melted white chocolate. Pull them out and place them on a plate.
9. Allow them to harden in the fridge for 5 minutes before enjoying your yummy treat.

MINI GARDEN PIE

INGREDIENTS

- ➤ 3 tablespoons of finely crushed Oreos for the crust, plus
- ➤ 3 tablespoons of crushed oreos for the top
- ➤ 1 tablespoon of melted butter
- ➤ 2 teaspoons of cream cheese
- ➤ 1 tablespoon of powdered sugar
- ➤ 4 tablespoons of chocolate or vanilla pudding
- ➤ 3-4 gummy worms

INSTRUCTIONS

1. Preheat your toy oven and spray your cooking pan with nonstick cooking oil.
2. In a small bowl, mix butter and 3 tablespoons of finely crushed Oreos together.
3. Spread the Oreo and butter mixture into the pan.
4. Bake your pan for 7 minutes in your toy oven.
5. Remove from the oven when it's finished baking and set aside to cool.
6. Now you can make the filling. Mix the cream cheese and powdered sugar together. Add in the pudding and mix well.
7. Pour the mixture onto the pan, and spread it over the pie crust.
8. Arrange your gummy worms on top so that they look like they're in a mini garden.
9. Layer the remaining 3 tablespoons of crushed Oreos on top of the pudding and around the gummy worms.
10. You can hide your gummy worms underneath the crushed Oreos with just their heads peaking out to make them look like they're buried in a tiny garden.

Made in the USA
Las Vegas, NV
14 September 2023